When Did You Last Se

Jeremy Hardy is one of the most original and popular of the new generation of stand-up comedians to have emerged in recent years and he commands huge and ecstatic audiences in venues all over Britain. He was acclaimed as the Top Stand-Up Live Comedy Performer in the British Comedy Awards for 1991. He has performed in venues throughout Britain and Ireland including the Edinburgh Festival Fringe and London's Bloomsbury Theatre and Hackney Empire. He lives in London.

When Did You Last See Your Father?

being a parent: how men do it

JEREMY HARDY

with photographs by Kit Hollerbach and Fred Sanjar

Mandarin

by the same author

Jeremy Hardy Speaks to the Nation

A Mandarin Humour Paperback

WHEN DID YOU LAST SEE YOUR FATHER?

First published in Great Britain in 1992
by Methuen London
First published in paperback by Mandarin
an imprint of Reed Consumer Books Ltd
Michelin House, 81 Fulham Road, London SW3 6RB
and Auckland, Melbourne, Singapore and Toronto

A CIP catalogue record for this book
is available at the British Library

ISBN 0 7493 1355 2

Printed in England by Clays Ltd, St Ives plc

Dedicated to
my wife Kit
and my daughter Betty

Special thanks to Geoffrey Strachan,
Paul B. Davies, Kit Hollerbach, Fred Sanjar,
Hannah Moore, Ben Keaton, Simon Clarke,
Dianne Sandler, Joe Sandler-Clarke,
Tim O'Dell, Mikki Loebner, Ella Loebner-
O'Dell and Sally Jones.

Contents

Introduction:
How Did I Come
to Write This Book?

How did I come to write a book? Well, like many of the great works of literature, it began as a chance remark. I was enjoying lunch with a publisher from Methuen when he happened to say, 'I'd like you to write a book.' Then he said, 'I can't make a formal offer at this moment but, subject to agreement by the editorial board, I can ring you later today to offer a commission and discuss the advance.'

At the time, I thought nothing of it, but some considerable time after that, something happened to jog my memory.

'Well?' said the publisher.

'I'm sorry?' I rejoindered.

'Do you want to write a book?'

'Book?'

'Look, please don't waste my time; I'm a very busy man.'

'Oh, I'm sorry, I was up all night with the baby.'

At this, the publisher became very agitated.

'Wait a minute, what was that you just said?'

'I can't remember.'

'Something about being up all night with the baby.'

'What baby?'

'Fatherhood! That's it – a book about fatherhood! What a great idea!'

I can't recall the rest of the conversation because by this time I was face down in my spaghetti *al vongole*. But months later, I was enjoying a late supper with my wife when she turned to me and said, 'Do you have to floss your teeth while we're eating? And you'd better start writing that book or they'll be getting cross with you. You've had fifteen hundred quid off them, remember.'

'Oh, Christ, I knew there was something,' I replied.

And so it was that I sat down to write my first book. And what better time to write a book about fatherhood? Had I tackled this subject in the late 1980s, I would have been condemned for cynically jumping on the parenting bandwagon to cash in on *en vogue* subject matter. Now, the worst I can be accused of is having woefully missed the boat.

But less about me, and more about my book. It is in no way intended to be the definitive or complete guide for today's fathers. Rather it is a random series of ill-informed notions and non-sequential ramblings with no real focus or point – but I like it. I hope that in years to come it will take its place alongside other books, or those things for keeping books standing up when they're not wedged against a wall.

Special Author's Note

During the course of this book where I have referred to a child of no particular sex, I have used the female pronoun 'she', rather than 'he' or 'it'. However, I have also used 'she' when talking specifically about a girl. I have also used 'he' when referring specifically to a boy, sometimes. I don't think I've used 'he' to describe a child of no particular sex, but I may have used it to describe a girl. I may also have used 'they' sometimes, which gets confusing because it's not clear whether it means a person of no particular sex or more than one person of the same or different sexes or indeed which sex I'm talking about. Sometimes I just get confused and say things which are a mistake. The reader must decide for him/herself whether s/he chooses to interpret 'he', 'she' or 'they' in one way or another. I don't think I've used 'it', but I may have done. Come to think of it, I think there's a bit where I did use 'he' to mean a child of no particular sex, but I can't for the life of me remember where. That's going to annoy me all day now.

Part One

Fatherhood and You

1 'I Want to be a Dad'

Why does a man want a child? Is it to prove that he has had sex at least once? Is it to perpetuate the species? Is the child a pet substitute?

Some scientists believe that every man is genetically programmed to procreate. That instinct, it is argued, combines with the male's almost limitless supply of ejaculate to produce a strong motivation toward impregnating females. This hypothesis provides the basis for the theory that men have a biological justification for wanting to do it all the time.

An instinctive drive to reproduce would also explain men's traditionally lackadaisical attitude to birth control. But do men have such an imperative and, if they do, is it instinctive and, if so, are they different from women in this respect and, if they are, how, and what do we mean by how?

The American social anthropologist, Myra Belsinger says:

> Women feel a social, psychological, peer-group and folkloric, as well as biological pressure to conceive, bear and nurture children, whereas men are just bastards.[1]

The conservative sociobiologist Dr Bernard O'White of the Department of Men's Studies at Harvard University believes in a profound genetic contrast between men and women which he explains using the cerebral diagrams shown on the next page.

[1] *Reproductivity and Carer-Oriented Maternity in a Patriarchal Oligarchy* (Harmony Books, 1987).

Fig. 1 Male Brain

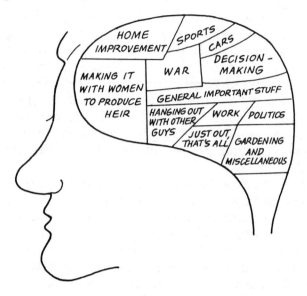

Fig. 2 Female Brain

But if men do have an innate will to 'make babies', why aren't they even more eager to 'hide the sausage'? Man's sex drive is believed to be sublimated by other activities and hobbies. Belsinger argues, for example, that aggressive driving is a typically male displacement activity. 'The automobile,' she writes, 'is merely a substitute phallus.' But if this were so, why would men drive too fast? Surely they would just back in and out of the garage – or maybe just polish the car a lot.[1]

Does man's appetite for sex betray a more profound, subconscious urge to father children, or are men just dirty? And what of gay men? The lack of desire to have sex with women doesn't necessarily mean a man doesn't want to be a father. Many gay men become fathers and this is not always because they are seeking cover in a seemingly 'normal' domestic situation. Indeed, there are gay men who would like to adopt but cannot fulfil the criterion of being a recently-castrated, married, middle-class consultant paediatrician and qualified social worker (see *Chapter 3: Adoption*).

Society tends to feel that homosexuality, unless rigorously disguised by ordination into the priesthood or election to the House of Commons, will be a 'bad influence' on a child. That is, it will make children homosexual. There is no evidence, however, to suggest that sexual preference is learned from parents. If one is heterosexual, it is not because one's parents were heterosexual. To a child, heterosexuality seems to be something not so much to do with sex but to do with arguing and shopping. And if, for example, one has a gay father, the main difference is that there is less arguing and more shopping.

In any event, there would seem to be a paternal instinct even when there is no search for a female partner. There comes a time for many men when the

[1] For further reading, see Belsinger's *The Erection – an Extension of the Penis* (Harmony Books, 1976).

restless stirrings of youth give way to a deeper yearning. A man wants a new person in this life, a person to whom he can say, 'One day all this will be yours' . . . 'Well, son it's like this' . . . 'Because I said so, that's why' . . . and 'I don't know, go and ask your mother.'

A man who has no children can feel a failure, especially if he has lost them somewhere. To whom will he explain the finer points of the googly and the difference between right and wrong? And who will show him how the video works? A man wants to sow his seed, pass on the family name, bring forth the next generation, sire a young 'un.

Belsinger argues that this is simply a desire to impress. It is considered socially normal for a married man to be a father and for an unmarried man to be seeking the future mother of his children. Belsinger is right that the approval men receive as fathers is different from the congratulation to be expected by mothers. A woman who has given birth is held to have done only what her body was designed for but the man who impregnated her is held to have *achieved* something. If the man were to give birth himself, there would be cause for such adulation. But the penis is impossibly designed for the delivery of a seven- or eight-pound human being. Then again, so is the vagina.

Why then has a man's status traditionally increased through fatherhood when a woman's has decreased through motherhood? Partly, it would seem, because as the head of a traditional family, a man was admired by his peers for the ability to raise several healthy children without ever actually seeing them. This is still the case with the higher social classes. It is often observed that the socially deprived are more likely than the wealthy to abuse their children. This is because the wealthy send their children away to be abused by professionals.

Increasingly, however, men of all social classes play a role in parenting their children and may incur resentment rather than praise from their peer group. Among young men, there exists a mythology about the dread onset of fatherhood. Clichés abound to the effect that new dads are no fun any more, never go out, are boring, show photographs all the time, look ill and smell funny. All these negative images are completely accurate and yet, fatherhood gives a man something. It is an affirmation of manhood in the eyes of the world. A man needs to establish to his society that he is a man. He could just go around showing his genitals to people. Many men do, indeed, opt for this course of action.

So what does the child, as distinct from the *fact* of the child represent, and when and which? Do men think that they *own* their offspring in the way that they might own a dog? If so, why don't they let their kids defecate outside other people's homes? What's more, one can hardly imagine an obedient child being trained to run to the newsagent and come back with the paper in her mouth. It's much more likely to be cigarettes. But prospective mothers should hear alarm bells if the father's favourite girl's name is Lady and boy's name is Lucky.[1]

Of course, children bear no resemblance to dogs, apart from the fact that they destroy everything, take over your life, bite and pretend to be deaf when they have their backs to you. But we do seem to spend a great deal of time yelling at children, ordering them about, stopping them from having their fun and getting a vicarious thrill from their attacks on other people.

So does fatherhood represent real as well as symbolic power? Is a child just someone else to push around? If so, fathers should bear in mind who it is who will be selecting sheltered accommodation for them when their own bladder control starts to go haywire.

In earlier centuries, children had greater *economic* significance. They were considered to be a financial asset because they were part of the workforce. In some areas of the world, children still labour for little or no

[1] For further reading, see *Men Who Throw Sticks For Their Children* by Prof Anthony Sligo (Trinity Publications, 1987).

reward in tough and dangerous conditions with no legal protection (see *Youth Training*, page 760).

But perhaps the one thing that all men seek from a child is a renewal of their own lives. Perhaps we all want a little replica of ourself and becoming a father is an easier way of doing this than becoming a major historical figure in order to be included in the Airfix range. And is it a bad thing to want to create a new person who looks a bit like you? Well, that depends on what you look like. Phil Collins, for example, would be best left as a one-off. However, to see some slight reflection of yourself in the face of an infant can be warmly reassuring, especially if you are not entirely convinced that you are the child's real father. But there is no guarantee that your child will look like you (see *Chapter 3: Adoption*). What a man seeks from a child is not so much a copy of himself as a continuation of his existence. We want to be immortal. We want to know that, even after we are gone, there will still be a little piece of us, somewhere on the Earth, who hates our guts.

2 Becoming a Dad

There is more than one way to skin a cat. The question 'Where do babies come from?' has vexed generations of biologists. Let's get one thing straight from the start: you can't get pregnant from sitting on a lavatory seat. Well, not if you're a man, anyway. If you're a woman, it depends on what you're doing while you're sitting on a lavatory seat.

Early scientists believed that it was the stork who delivered babies. The reason for this fallacy is the fact that storks have a large pouch of skin for carrying food, which hangs under their beak – or is that pelicans? Anyway, the stork was a powerful symbol of fertility to the ancient Cretans of the Minoan dynasty. According to legend, Sinbad the Sailor Man slew King Solomon while he was hiding in the oak tree burning the spider. Grieving for her dead husband, Queen Maeve turned into a stork in order to hide the child she was carrying from the Canaanites. When the infant prince was born, she flew down from her nest on top of Mount Atari and left the boy with a barren woman who was making things for tourists. Zeus proclaimed that, henceforth, any mortal who wished to have a child should make offerings to the Stork Queen that she might grant their wish. The Minoans died out. The legend, however, survived. You can still hear stories like this on Crete, especially if you ask an English tour guide why your plane has been delayed for twenty-four hours.

Today, we know that the stork does not bring babies because storks are colour-blind and would be unable to tell whether to dress them in pink or blue. Neither is it the case that one can find babies under a gooseberry bush. For this myth, we have good old Saxon vulgarity to thank. The origin of the misapprehension is linguistic. 'Gooseberry bush' in this context is actually a corruption of *Knootzbergenspeltzhabusch*, a Norse word meaning lavatory seat or stork.

The main contenders among competing explanations today are freak winds, aliens, demonic possession and sexual intercourse. As implied in the previous chapter, the last one is probably the most common cause.

The majority of us, at some time in our lives, engage in what's called 'the sexual act', but most of the time we're too drunk to remember much about it. Of course, it's wrong to see sex just as a means of producing a child. Sex is an integral part of being close to someone and giving mutual pleasure in a loving relationship. And it gives you something to think about when you're masturbating.

There are alternative ways of combining the male and female units of reproduction but coitus is undeniably a very practical route to conception for many people. However, for men who choose this method, there are a number of hurdles to clear first.

Finding someone who's prepared to go to bed with you

For some men, this can seem the easiest thing in the world, or so they would have you believe. For others, it's a painful journey of discovery. Here are some men's experiences in their own words:

> 'Yup, I'm pretty successful with women. The girl I'm seeing at the moment is terrific but not just her looks. She's got like a personality and everything, you know; she's a real laugh. If you can make a girl laugh, you're halfway there. I'm a real lunatic anyway. Often girls say they think I'm really crazy but I've been feeling much better lately and I've got my own flat now. I reckon I'm

pretty good-looking and everything but for most girls that's not what it's about. It's about having a laugh with them. Karen just falls about every time I suggest sex. Then she leaves.'

Dave, engineering student, 20

'Most girls just want a good time and that's fine with me. They're after sex as much as we are, only I think men are just more honest about it. Girls don't like wimpy guys, they want men to be strong. And that's not sexist. I mean, Christine, this girl I'm seeing at the moment, she can give as good as she gets. In fact, last night, she kept jabbing me in the pelvis with a blunt pencil.'

Tom, advertising copywriter, 23

'If I see a girl and I want to go to bed with her, I suddenly start convulsing and bleeding from the ears. That way, she gets the message.'

Steve, salesman, 34

'I don't have a very active sex life as such. I have a lot of close women friends who don't think about me in that way and I think that's very supportive. In particular, I have one special platonic girlfriend and sometimes I sense a real sexual chemistry between us, but she says having sex would "spoil things". Spoil her sex life, I suppose. She says that she feels like a sister to me. So she breaks things and then blames me for it. I told her I used to have baths with my sisters but she told me not to be stupid.'

Mike, community artist, 28

In other words, finding someone you want to go to bed with and finding someone who wants to go to bed with you are two different things. Finding someone you want to go to bed with who also wants to go to bed with you is something else again. Many of us spend a large part of our lives with no more carnal gratification than the shower-fittings page of the Argos catalogue.

It is true, however, that people become sexually active at a much younger age than they did ten or twenty years ago. When I was fourteen, 'sex with a condom' meant sex *with* a condom – nobody else was involved. But, although young men may be having more sex than their predecessors did, that does not mean that they are in search of fatherhood. A man is much more likely to want children when he has already been through several relationships which ended because he did not want to have children. This gives added urgency to his search for a suitable partner. At this point, the message is: DON'T PANIC! Men are fortunate in that they can remain sexually potent and fertile until long after they are dead.

Nevertheless, waiting for the right girl to come along can be frustrating and disappointing, and there are positive steps which a man can take. Try begging women to sleep with you or inventing a tragic personal history. You might also opt for corrective surgery or pretending to be someone else. Good luck, and remember: DON'T PANIC!

'We've done it – now what?'

If you've only had sex with someone once, it's unlikely that you've made her pregnant, unless both of you are under seventeen. You may have to sustain quite a long relationship before a woman conceives. Despite all the passion and excitement that marks the start of a romance, there can be a rocky road ahead. If you're serious about wanting a relationship to last, you have to work at it. To this end, try undermining her self-confidence so that she comes to feel dependent on you and stays with you out of insecurity.

'The Right Time'

You may have been with someone for some time. You may even be married. But if a happy accident has not occurred, DON'T PANIC! It's time to discuss things with your partner. Tell her how you feel. Reassure her that wanting a child doesn't mean that you feel there's anything missing from the relationship. Threaten to kill yourself. *Don't,* however, try to become pregnant yourself. Nine times out of ten, this leads to further disappointment and frustration and for the lucky minority of men who do conceive, there are no courtelle slacks with elasticated waistbands which are long enough in the leg.

So what makes women pregnant?

About sperms

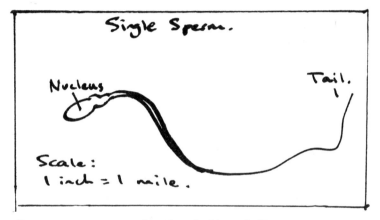

Sperms are not, as is often believed, living creatures. They are actually fossils of tiny snakes which became extinct during the Ice Age. They cannot, of course, be seen by the naked eye because they come out too fast. Once inside the liver, they meet eggs, go out with them and make them pregnant. It is these pregnant eggs which give birth to embryos. The embryonic phase of development is a pupal stage. The embryo lives off the sperms which failed to get off with an egg and grows until it becomes a chrysalis. In turn, the lava sheds its winter coat and migrates to the uterus. This is what we mean by menstruation.

There are, however, ways of stopping this process from taking place and ways of encouraging it.

FRONT BOTTOM OF LADY.

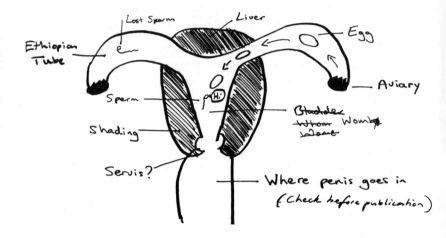

FRONT BOTTOM OF MAN

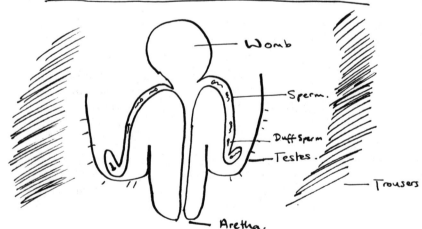

Trying for a family

This can be a long and dispiriting business, especially for men who are not having sex with anyone. But if you are having sex with someone, there are things you can do to increase the likelihood of fertilisation.

Your sperm count can be adversely affected by heat, caffeine and alcohol, so try to avoid soaking your testicles in Irish coffee before sex.

Stress can also be a problem, so try not to make your sperms feel that they have to compete with one another. Remember: it's not a race.

Diet is also very important: you are what you eat! Eating sperm will not, however, make you more fertile, unless you are very underweight. A healthy diet will contain a balance of foods to provide all the nutrients you need but will make you very depressed because there won't be any chocolate or biscuits in it.

Worrying certainly isn't going to help matters, but if it makes you feel better, you may as well keep doing it for the sake of your peace of mind.

Your partner

Many women can tell if they are ovulating by the texture of their mucus, so get your partner to blow her nose before sex and have a look. If this does not work, which it won't, she can try using a thermometer, although a penis is usually more effective. She may be able to calculate when her ovulations should take place by looking at her diary or calendar. If she finds a date when she has an important job interview, that will be the day when her period starts and she can work it out from that. It's important not to waste your goes by doing it on the wrong days because then you'll just start enjoying yourselves and forget what you're supposed to be doing it for.

'Is it me?'

For most men, it is hard to accept the idea that there may be something wrong with their sperm, other than the fact that it's very hard to clean off a suede jacket. The important thing to remember here is: DON'T PANIC! The best course of action is to get your GP or someone who knows a bit about medicine to refer you to a subfertility clinic and arrange to have your semen analysed.

You will be given a small plastic flask. This has the word 'sterile' on it which isn't very encouraging. You will also be given an instruction manual – manual being the operative word at this point. The instructions will tell you not to have an ejaculation for four days before producing your sample. That is because, after four days without an ejaculation, you will quite fancy the small plastic flask. This is where you must direct your ejaculation.

It can be a good idea to involve your partner. She probably has a good idea of what you're going through and wants to support you if she can. Don't feel it's *your* problem, even though it is. You must share things with your partner and not go off into your own world, leaving her feeling powerless to help. I thought it would be good to get my wife to help 'start me off'. She did this by managing to get the lid off the flask. But it can be awkward and humiliating trying to reach a climax and aim your ejaculation into a little plastic container so you might ask your partner to assist you with this by holding the flask and running around after you trying to catch it. Try to make the experience fun. Perhaps invite a few close friends around and tell them to bring their cameras.

Once your sample is safely in the flask, put the lid on very tightly. It's vital that you don't lose any of the sample through leakage because it can leave you look-ing very silly on the bus. If you only manage to produce a tiny amount of sperm, make up the difference with a little natural yoghurt or wallpaper paste. It's also important that your sample reaches the clinic while it's still warm so, on arrival at the hospital, ask the canteen staff to heat it up in a saucepan or pop it in the microwave for a couple of minutes.

When you hand the sample in at the clinic, don't feel embarrassed. Hospital personnel are well used to receiving samples and, believe me, you could be giving them far worse things than semen, although it is best not to. There is nothing to be ashamed of; you are taking a mature and responsible attitude and exercising control over the question of your fertility. The staff will respect this and show consideration. They will simply ask for your name. Don't tell them, though, because you don't want people thinking you're weird. It's generally best to make up a name or use the name of a friend you don't like very much.

What are they looking for?

In a word: sperms. The analyst will conduct a *sperm count*. To do this he has to catch and ring the sperms, or *spermatozoa*. This is quite painless and the sperms often see it as a game. When the total is added up, the clinic will be able to tell you your sperm count. If they tell you that it is normal, they may be lying to spare your feelings, so get a second opinion. If, however, your count is low or non-existent, you have a fertility problem. This is not the same thing as being impotent. It does not affect your ability to perform sexually, but it does mean that you've been leaping off the wardrobe onto your partner holding a stopwatch and a wall-planner for no very good reason. There is no point, however, in tormenting yourself about the fact that, for the last six months, all the romance and spontaneity have been taken out of sex by your efforts to have a child – or the fact that, for years before that, all the romance and spontaneity were taken out of sex by your efforts *not* to have a child, which seem signally futile now. Several missed opportunities may haunt you for the rest of your life.

By far the worst thing about finding out that you can't have children is that the person you will probably find out from will be a *hospital receptionist* – or 'border guard' as they are called in hospitals with trust status. (In my view, hospital receptionists should not be given the job of imparting delicate information to people because they do not have interpersonal skills. They should be working underground, without light or air.) There may be no preparatory phone call from them, no appointment with your consultant, they'll probably just shout your results from an open window when you're walking past one day.

Initially, you will be devastated. Then you will try to think of a positive angle on your situation and comfort yourself with phrases like 'What kind of a world is it to bring a child into anyway?' This, however, is poor consolation because it means that, not only have you got no children, you've got a crap planet as well.

This all sounds very bleak, but the battle isn't lost yet. It is unlikely that you have no sperms. You probably just don't have very many, or it may be that your sperms are non-swimmers. If this is the case, it may be possible for doctors to artifically inseminate your partner with your sperm using a technique called FITTBA, which stands for Firing It up There with a Turkey Baster. If, however, there is no way that your partner can be fertilised by your sperm, you may be looking for a donor.

Someone else's semen

Many people carry a semen donor card. In the event of their having an accident, their sperm can be used to help someone who needs it. Alternatively, you can go to your nearest sperm bank and ask to see the Small Business Adviser. Hospitals also take donations from volunteers but, unfortunately, these donors are often medical students so there is a greater than average risk of mental abnormality.

If you do use donated sperm, it is important not to feel that the donor is the 'real father'. A real father is a man who loves and cares for children and helps to bring them up. This means that most people in history have been illegitimate.

You may decide to find a donor from among your friends or family. Ask your partner if there's anyone she'd particularly like to have sex with and then pay for them to go on holiday together. Alternatively, you can hire a private detective to visit someone and dupe them into providing some sperm by posing as a person conducting a survey on masturbation.

IVF

In vitro fertilisation is a developing field. It is a relatively-new and exciting branch of medicine which means the drugs haven't been tested properly. It is not, however, as much like science fiction as it sounds. Test-tube babies are not born in laboratories unless, that is, the maternity wing has run out of beds. Eggs are removed from a woman and mixed with sperm outside the body. If fertilisation takes place, the embryos are either reimplanted into the womb or, in the case of wealthy parents, sent straight to boarding school.

Whatever your reproductive situation, good luck and DON'T PANIC!

3 Adoption

I have a special interest in this subject because my own parents were adopted and have spent most of their lives trying to find out who their natural children are.

For centuries, there has been a stigma attached to adoption. People choosing to bring up a child who was not theirs by birth were made to feel freakish, inadequate and unnatural by society. But times have changed and it is now the role of adoption agencies to make them feel like that.

How easy is it to adopt?

It used to be the case that there were huge numbers of unwanted babies in Britain and that the screening of would-be adopters was quite relaxed. Today, birth control and single parenthood have reduced the numbers dramatically, so the adoption authorities aim to ensure that those children who *are* unwanted stay in care for as long as possible. To this end, the process of adoption is as tortuous and incomprehensible as British Rail's discount policy.

There are now very few *babies* available for adoption. Homes are needed, however, for a large number of older children, including teenagers, many of whom were babies when the paperwork on their cases was started.

What are the authorities looking for in adopters?

It is now accepted that the fact of having been in care is very much a part of the child's identity and that, if placed with a family, the child is cut off from institutionalised life. Recognising this problem of cultural adjustment and the need for a child to be kept in touch with his or her origins, adoption agencies are keen for children to be placed only with families whose homes have a strong smell of disinfectant and whose cooking is as bland and unpleasant as possible.

Preference is also given to younger couples. Agencies are aware that people over thirty-five generally suffer from memory loss and knock things over all the time. There is also a problem of relating. The guidance given to agencies by the Department of Health and Social Security on this matter is as follows:

> Teenagers with parents in their fifties are apt to find them 'square' and not tuned in to the with-it scene of the young moderns which is very much the 'in thing', apparently. It is, therefore, recommended that couples should adopt only from within their own age group. Ideally, they will be slightly younger than the child.[1]

Many adoption agencies require you to be married. This is because it is felt that a child who has, in effect, been abandoned by its natural parents, needs the stability and security of a couple whose relationship consists of talking about tiling and discount kitchen furniture. The requirement of marriage also means that adoption agencies can exclude lesbian and gay couples, without having to own up to the fact that they think homosexuals shouldn't be allowed near children because they might give them funny ideas.

As well as being young, heterosexual and married, it helps considerably if you or your partner have fertility problems:

> A couple who have adopted and then go on to have a child of their own will inevitably dump the adopted one in a skip. You know what people are like.[2]

[1] *Circular on Adoption and Placement* (DHSS, 1986).
[2] National Agencies for Adoption and Fostering (Annual Report, 1990).

For a man, therefore, you will need to submit a letter from your subfertility clinic or proof that you have been interrogated by the West Midlands police. Women should have the word 'Barren' branded on their foreheads. It is important, however, that you are not perceived as making an irrational decision based on grief about your childlessness. The adoption panel assessing your application will want to be satisfied that you have come to terms with it. Try to find an Enjoying Infertility workshop in your area and enrol.

Adopting a child places great demands on yourself and your relationship with your partner. Social workers will need to know that you can cope with the sudden arrival into your life of a strange and possibly disturbed individual. So they will often turn up without telephoning first.

You must be patient during the months of assessment. Social workers are highly trained and qualified. They are not there to make you feel humiliated or persecuted – they just can't help themselves. There is no point in losing your temper; a professional social worker is well used to deflecting anger. Here are the words of a would-be adopter unable to deal with the stress of being assessed:

'It had been ten months. We had been cooperating as fully as we could. We'd had all the medical exams and police checks and supplied Roger with photographs of ourselves naked as the agency requested. We'd even started to quite enjoy the preparatory Sensory Deprivation Sessions for Prospective Adopters. But one day I snapped. It was five o'clock on Christmas morning and Lisa was still very groggy and sore after the hysterectomy she'd been told to have. I was bringing her in a cup of tea when Roger knocked on the back door. When I opened it, I thought he just wanted to see Lisa's scar, but he said, 'Charlie, look Clarice and I have split. I need to crash here for a few days.' I took the vacuum cleaner from the cupboard and began beating him in the face. I thought that, after a while, he would lose consciousness

but he just kept saying, "Charlie, you're channelling
your energy in a very unproductive way."'

Adopting from abroad

Most agencies are ideologically opposed to intercountry
adoption. To quote Marjory St Ivel, chair of the National Agencies for Adoption and Fostering:

'Everyone has seen pictures of pathetic-looking, unwanted children in other countries, but the desire to try
to help them by adoption is misplaced. By far the best
place for a child to grow and develop is in its own country,
with its own kind, that is, people of its own ethnic group,
who can relate to its experience and sense of rhythm.
How would it feel, for example, to be of South American
origin and never to know what it is to do the samba or be
gunned down by a right-wing death squad? Children
need to belong and are likely to feel isolated in a culture
where they stand out as being different, whereas back
where they belong they all look the same to me. . . . I
mean there's a continuity, er . . . What is more, the
young are the future of their country. Children's homes
turn out the psychiatric patients of tomorrow and tomorrow belongs to me. Am I making any sense? Anyway,
charity begins at home, that's what I say.'[1]

There is also opposition from the Home Office:

Many of these children are not genuinely orphaned.
They are *economic* orphans. In our own economic situation, there is great competition for jobs and it is unreasonable to expect children here to want to share their
paper rounds with children from abroad. Giving foreign
nationals the right to residence will, therefore, only
serve to increase racial tension among babies and young
children.[2]

[1] In an interview with the author.
[2] *Circular on Childless Weirdos Who Want to Buy Up All These
Snot-Nosed Foreign Kids and Bring Them in by the Back Door*
(Home Office, 1991).

If you want to adopt a child from overseas, you will have to do it without much help from authority. You may also find yourself surprised by the attitudes you come across in the ordinary way. This is especially true if you do not already have children. When you see or hear the word 'childless', it generally means, 'broken, desperate, lizard-people with no genitals, who will stop at nothing to grab a baby from somewhere.' You may find that your story becomes widely known in your community and that other parents in the supermarket wheel their tots away from you in case you try to snatch them and pay for them at the checkout.

Even quite close friends may ask questions like these:

'So, how much did it cost to have her real parents murdered?'

'Intercountry adoption? Is that when they buy a Turkish man's kidneys, transplant them into your sperm and you give birth on behalf of an American couple?'

'How much darker do you think she'll get?'

People who are rather more socially aware may well ask you what efforts you are making to teach her about her own culture, to which a useful reply is, 'Probably more than you – I don't see your little Jack doing much morris dancing in his Bart Simpson shell-suit.'

Try to ignore people who ask you about genetics and who believe that, even if the child you adopt is a baby, she will inevitably start to exhibit innate foreign behaviour patterns at some point in the future. Imagine that you yourself had been adopted from Britain as a baby by a foreign couple, and spent all your life in a peasant village, working the land, and speaking the language of that country. Then, ask yourself whether you think it likely that at the age of thirty, you would suddenly find yourself saying, 'Very mild today, isn't it?'

After adoption

If you adopt a child who is too young to understand what's happening, it is vital that you don't try to hide the fact of her adoption from her – unless you think you can get away with it. It's also best if the child can assimilate the idea over a period of time. Springing it on her the morning of her driving test is probably not a good idea. Ideally, she will hear the word 'adopted' used quite frequently from the start, although it's not a concept that's easy for a child to grasp, so you may want to supplement it with more tangible phrases like, 'I am not your real father' or 'You were abandoned by a wicked lady.'

Even if your child is old enough to know that she is being adopted, don't think it's a subject to ignore. Make it a special and celebrated fact. Talk about it openly and freely. How often you should mention it will depend on how badly behaved your child is.

At some stage, the child will want to know more about her natural parents and may want to trace and meet them. You must not feel that this means you've failed as a parent. All children are spiteful and ungrateful to the people who've slaved and made sacrifices for them. It's a way of asserting their development towards independence, although they're not so independent when it comes to borrowing the car, or buying a pair of trainers they'll wear once and then leave lying around for you to fall over.

If you have adopted from abroad and fail to explain things thoroughly to your child, she may feel insecure, confused or fearful that she might be sent away again. Of course, a legally-adopted child cannot be deported, but she doesn't have to know that.

Social services will want to know that you are taking steps to keep the child in touch with her cultural heritage. It is a good idea, for example, for the child to have access to the literature and music of her home country. If she is from South America, you are fortunate in that Latin folk music is very fashionable and widely available in Britain, although if you were to visit the mountains of Peru, you'd probably find that everyone's trying to get hold of Shakin' Stevens' records. If, however, you have a child from Eastern Europe, you won't find a large selection in the HMV 'World Music' rack, but you may have luck in picking up various artefacts, especially as all the good stuff in Eastern Europe is exported for hard currency.

It is, however, very negative and destructive for a child to grow up with the idea that she comes from a country which is cruel and uncivilised and where people don't care about children, so you may as well come clean and tell her that she wasn't born in Britain.

As she gets older you might even want to learn some of the language of the country where she was born. It can be great fun being able to talk to your child in her native language because, of course, she won't understand what you're saying.

There's been an awful lot to take on board in this chapter but, if you decide you'd like to become an adoptive father, good luck and DON'T PANIC!

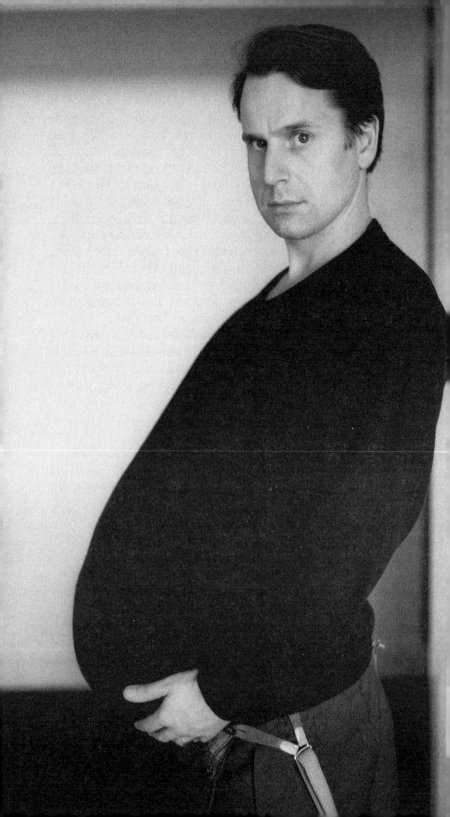

4 Pregnancy and Birth

DON'T PANIC! A man who becomes a father by means of his partner becoming pregnant can find the experience every bit as rewarding as adoption.

But if this does happen to you, you may find yourself prone to extra emotional stresses and upheavals. Up until now, it's been a joint effort and now it can seem like your job is over. Matters will take their own course regardless of you. You feel redundant. All eyes are on the mother-to-be and your role in things is forgotten. It seems as if no one is taking account of your apprehension and dramatic mood swings. Yet all these emotions are completely natural, if you are a bleating milksop.

Don't feel that there's nothing for you to do during the pregnancy. Go out and get drunk a lot – it's your last chance for a good while. You might think that, in order to help your partner to abstain from alcohol during her pregnancy, you should do the same, but making yourself miserable isn't going to help her. On the contrary, developing a very large, rotund abdomen yourself is a good way of making her feel less self-conscious, and throwing up every morning will enable you to share in some of the feelings of being pregnant.

Talking

You may be experiencing considerable anxiety. Childbirth is an awe-inspiring event and a lot to take on board. There may be financial worries. Babies are very expensive and where you're living may not be a great place to have a child. You're not sure if you or your finances can cope. You may also be having misgivings about all the changes that will inevitably take place in your life, and what fatherhood will really *be like*.

It's very important not to share any of these feelings with your partner. She's got enough to worry about without you telling her that you're about to be made redundant or that there's a history of mental illness in your family. Just tell her nothing's wrong and drink more. If you've taken to stealing, invent an aunt who's left you some money or a lot of car stereos.

Sex during pregnancy

It is really too late for this. Once conception has taken place, having sex again isn't going to make any difference, so it's a fairly pointless exercise. Even if you want to have a second or third child, it's best to wait until after the first baby is born before trying for another – a minimum of four or five minutes is recommended. If, however, you want to have *twins* and they don't show up on the first scan, it might be worth having one more go before it's too late.

It may be, however, that you wish to continue having sex for religious reasons. If so, you might want to wait for a few months. You probably won't feel like sex when your partner first becomes pregnant because you'll have done it so much in the last year. As for her, all the nausea and vomiting will leave her feeling quite unsexy, so it's best to lay off the drink for a while if you do want her to do it with you.

You may be nervous that penetrating your partner will damage the baby. In this case, you should talk to your GP who will examine you and either set your mind at rest or suggest that you enter a competition.

Some men feel unattractive during pregnancy but only if they were unattractive beforehand. Your partner may also need some reassurance. Try telling her that you find the gravid turn of her belly and heavy, blue-veined breasts very sexy, although she'll probably think you're weird.

Feelings of jealousy are very common; in the words of one prospective father:

'Theresa seemed so self-possessed, and although I knew my feelings were irrational, I felt somehow superfluous. I also became aware of possessive, territorial sensations I didn't know I was capable of. It was as if the inside of her had been mine in some way, and now there was someone else there. I asked the antenatal counsellor where all these emotions were coming from and she told me that Theresa was having an affair with one of the other dads.'

As the time of the birth approaches, it is wise to abstain from coital sex, particularly if you are in an ambulance. Pregnancy can, however, be a time of sexual discovery for couples. You may learn to express physical love and affection through greater touching and stroking, without feeling that full intercourse is everything, although it's more likely that you'll both just masturbate a lot more.

Getting ready for the event

There is such a bewildering array of goods and brands on the market that the prospective father can be quite perplexed about what to buy for his new baby! In general, it is best to choose small things. Babies are not very big and tend to be rather dwarfed by a double bed or size thirteen Dr Martens.

You can waste an awful lot of time and money if you're not absolutely clear what you will actually need. Below is a checklist which I hope is a useful guide:

    Clothes
    Bottles
    Nappies and that
    Other stuff

You will also need to go to classes and keep lots of towels boiling.

The birth

At some time, you and your partner will have to make decisions about the birth. Increasingly, many men decide that they want to be present at the birth – although very few women do. If you decide for whatever reason that you'd rather not witness the birth, suggest to your partner that someone else might take your place – a friend or relative, or maybe even a doctor or midwife if the hospital is unusually well staffed.

Delivery at home

Pizza is generally best, although a growing number of excellent Indian take-aways now offer a delivery service. You will both get very run-down and neglect to buy or prepare food for yourselves once the baby is born, and a nourishing meal need only be a phone call away. Remember, they are there to help.

Some women give birth at home. This is usually because of an unreliable minicab firm, but some couples *prefer* a home birth. For a father, it can allow him to take part in the delivery while at the same time not missing anything on television. There is no reason why babies should not be born at home providing you have the training and equipment for blood transfusions, resuscitation, incubation and Caesarean operations, and an unfailing conviction that all medical science is bunk because African women do it in the paddy-fields and then carry on dancing without any bother.

One advantage of home birth is that older children are able to witness the birth of their new baby brother or sister. This is a good way of making them feel involved in the new arrival and also traumatising them for the rest of their lives.

Couples often opt for a home birth after having had an unpleasant experience of hospital delivery. In the words of one father:

'Gina had been in labour for ninety-two hours when the doctor arrived. He was holding all these long, scary-looking implements, although the midwife reassured us that they were only his golf clubs. He asked her if there was any chance of a drink and then said to Gina, "Now then young lady, what seems to be the trouble?" Gina told him that she was giving birth and he said, "I'll be the judge of that." Then he said he wanted to bring in some students to examine her. She said it was okay because she didn't want to be difficult. It turned out that they were geography students. We had to make a donation for rag week before they would go away.'

Natural childbirth

You may decide that you wish your partner to suffer the worst agony known to humankind on the grounds that it's natural. Some men also like a mother to die in childbirth because it's part of our folk heritage.

Stella Danzigger in *The Joy of Pain*, writes:

> Few can deny that the complete satisfaction of having a child's head force its way out of your vagina is one of the most rewarding experiences in a woman's life. The bitter-sweet tearing of human flesh accompanied by the sound of your own screaming gives far more pleasure than any sensation-numbing drug.[1]

Danzigger argues that the best form of pain relief is the emotional support which a man can give to his partner in labour. If you want to offer encouragement in the delivery room, you might say things like, 'Hey, tremendous, you're really dilating beautifully,' to which she may well reply, 'Fuck off. If it wasn't for you, I wouldn't be here.'

Many fathers are now enthusiastic about the idea of active birth or alternative labour. If one looks at all the literature on the subject, it is quite clear that a lot of

[1] (Earthmother Books, 1989)

men prefer unconventional positions and environments for the birth of their child. It is also clear, however, that these men are ugly and have beards.

Some couples believe in recycling the placenta. It is an organ which contains all the nutrients which have sustained the foetus and some people who have a home birth cook and eat it as a way of celebrating the birth and benefiting from its goodness.

Adopters will obviously not have this option but they may wish to cook and eat the social worker as an alternative.

5 'Now I'm a Dad'

Congratulations. You're a father. All you've got to do now is bring up the child.

Choosing a name

Jeremy is probably the best name for a boy – Jeremella for a girl. The origin is biblical, deriving from the prophet Jeremiah. Biblical names are always favourites, although Herod, Judas and Sodom are to be avoided.

Also try to avoid a name which has been made temporarily fashionable by a film or TV series. If you've ever met a man called Spartacus, you'll know what I mean. Today, maternity wards are bursting with Kylies, Jasons, Sineads, Gazzas and Terminators.

Bear in mind that the child will have to live with the name for many years. Everyone you know will tell you of a Mr and Mrs Christmas who named their daughter Mary. Of course, these tales are often apocryphal but my own primary-school classmates included a Phyllis Stein, a Delia Cards, a Dave Reckoning and a Sol Ventabuse

There is also a vogue for inventing names for children. This dates back to the Summer of Love of 1967 but today, minor celebrities and the moderate Left still feel entitled to saddle their children with ridiculous names. In the parents' minds, this justifies the fact that they will later remove the child from a state school where she is being mercilessly brutalised for having such a stupid name. It will be for the child's protection that she is transferred to a private school where she can grow up alongside children with equally silly names.

Several names have class connotations; my own, for example. I was born on a council estate but once I'd been called Jeremy, we had to move. It may be, however, that you want your child to spend their life fending off violent attacks. In this case, the best name for a boy is Sue. Fans of the popular country singer Johnny Cash will remember that the Boy Named Sue grew up to be a pretty mean fighter. Sue is also a good name for a girl, although it does not produce the same effect since, technically, it is a girl's name. If you really want a fight to ensue every time your daughter is asked her name, it's best to call her simply, 'What's It To You, Fuckface?' It will certainly make for some lively beginnings at new schools and animated job interviews later on.

Choosing a sex

You must not seek to impose on your child your idea of what you want her sex to be. Babies are born sightless and covered in fur, and do not develop a gender until they are seven or eight years old. It is vital that you let the child determine her own sex at her own pace. Conditioning is very influential so clothes and names will affect the outcome. You may wish to choose an androgynous name like Frances, Leslie, Vivian or Dolores, so as not to steer the child unduly.

Feeding

During your partner's pregnancy her body will change. You will also notice that she has purchased a *breast-pump*. This is because she is pumping up her breasts so that they are big enough to fit the milk in.

Where a mother takes sole responsibility for feeding, the father may feel excluded and alienated but it is well worth it. Remember that the sleep you lose when your baby is young can never be regained. Even if you prefer the baby to have formula milk, this can be expressed into the breasts using the pump.

It is important that men do not feel pressurised into breast-feeding. It may just not be for you. If you do breast-feed, it is vital that you supplement the feeds with formula or your partner's milk, otherwise the baby will starve to death.

If your partner is having a hard time with breast-feeding try to encourage her with exhortations like, 'Don't you want him to have any immunities, then?' . . . 'You're not a proper woman' . . . and 'My mother breast-fed me till I was seven.' It is important that, if she does give up and change to bottle-feeding, she is made to feel guilty and a failure. Many books have been written to help you with this. To quote Stella Danzigger again:

> The single most rewarding thing in a woman's life is the lovely, hot, prickly spurting of her own milk through chapped and bleeding nipples, while a child bites on them. Anyway, I managed it, so I don't see why anyone else shouldn't.[1]

Weaning onwards

Getting a baby onto solids is a matter of experiment. A lot of very good books of advice about kids and food have been produced by people with nannies, and by the parents' pressure group Celebrity Housewives Who've Lost the Will to Live Against Food Additives.

Your health visitor and baby clinic will advise against packets and jars and tell you instead to simply 'purée some of what you're having'. The trouble is that Pizza Hut don't purée, unless, that is, the lad on the moped goes under a bus. In general, it is extremely reckless to purée some of what you're having and give it to a baby – lamb madras and half a bottle of Jameson at

[1] *Woman as Wet-Nurse – the Case for Slavery* (Earthmother Books, 1981).

two o'clock in the morning can sit very heavily on a tiny stomach.

Commercial baby foods are a mixture of good and bad. Don't be duped into thinking that the ones called things like Winter Vegetable Julienne with Braised Breast of Spring Chicken Mornay will be any less foul-tasting than the others. Look at the labels and avoid the ones whose lists of ingredients read, 'Water, dextrose, viscose, partially-adulterated vegetable fat, chlorine, salt, liver-shaped pieces, lard-extract, gluten, reconstituted dried water, herb-style flavours, vegetable lookalikes, shit.'

When children are older, you may want to try them with a few things that contain stabiliser, as this will help to stop them falling off their bikes. But, in general, be careful of additives. I gave my niece a chemistry set one Christmas, and by Easter, she was extracting the E numbers from chewing-gum and snorting them. Hi-tech foods and hi-tech children are a potent cocktail; today, if you give a seven-year-old a home computer, a Pot Noodle and some string, she can produce a small-scale nuclear device in two or three days.

I'm jumping ahead here. Baby starter-foods usually contain very little of anything and are unlikely to be dangerous. The food industry is very scrupulous in ensuring that anything which might harm infants is safely exported to developing countries.

There are not many things a little baby will eat, anyway. For older babies, whose tastes have become more sophisticated, there is a much wider choice of prepared meals available. My American in-laws are constantly amazed to see British supermarket shelves laden down with such a wide range of products. Many of the things we can buy here are simply not available in the States, having been banned many years ago for health reasons.

When Baby is onto 'finger foods', there are many old-favourite ruses for enticing babies and toddlers to take an interest in their meals. Fun shapes are a good idea:

try carving little pieces of cheese into the shape of ink pens or toilet brushes. Fill an icing-bag with mashed avocado or swede and spell out the words 'Keep out of the reach of children' or 'Warning: contains hydrochloric acid' on a sheet of greaseproof paper. If you have the time, decorate your child's mouth as if it were the cassette compartment of your video recorder and sit her in front of a mirror with a plate of sandwiches.

Hygiene

In general, there is universal agreement about the importance of keeping your child and your home very clean. Where controversy arises is over the question of disposable versus terry nappies.

It is hard to believe that, in the 1990s, after all that human beings have learned during the millennia of our tenure on this our Earth, there are people who campaign for a return to cloth nappies. It is even harder to comprehend how a person can be so bored that they devote any more than a passing thought to using cloth nappies, let alone trying to get other people to do it.

If there is a crisis over landfill sites in the United States and a depletion of forestry caused by paper-milling, I cannot think of a better reason for it than that Earth's space and resources are being devoted to dragging humankind out of the pit of barbarism that is terry nappies. Better that a thousand acres of trees are felled to provide Pampers than that a single, closely-typed sheet of A4 be devoted to expounding the virtues of pinning large towels around the crotches of children in order that they may use them as toilets.

Yes, it is true that you can save a lot of money by washing and reusing a terry nappy, but you could equally economise by not wiping your bottom and simply chipping the sediment off once a month with a chisel.

Furthermore, the heat energy and/or chemical pollutants that go into sterilising soiled nappies are no great boon to the environment and, to be frank, the environment isn't known for its consideration towards humans anyway. Nature never provided incubators or insulin; Nature provides earthquakes, volcanoes, mosquitoes, stinging-nettles, slugs, pain and death. And what a bitter irony that ninety per cent of books expressing concern about the planet are written by people who live on the San Andreas Fault. I think I make myself clear.

A dirty job

You must not show any revulsion for your baby's faeces. Experts agree that children should not feel inhibited about or ashamed of their excrement or that it is dirty or unpleasant. This is the opposite of the view which is taken about adults and their faeces, but I'm sure there's a good reason for it – probably something to do with potty-training and serial killers.

As to teaching a toddler to use the potty, kids learn by example. It can be hard for Dad to convince his tots that urine should go into a container, when most of *his* goes over the bathroom floor. However, a child adapts much better to passing *stools* into the potty since this enables her to take them out and use them as hair gel before you can stop her, or indeed video her doing it. If you do stop her, it's important not to say anything negative, like 'dirty' or 'bastard' – try something like, 'Okay, Harriet, there's a reason why we tend to feel it's not valid to wear those on our heads as such.'

If your child won't even get as far as defecating in the potty, line it with a piece of expensive carpet and this will almost certainly do the trick.

When the first stool does make it into the pot, your child will feel proud of herself and you should be equally delighted and encouraging. It can be a nice idea to freeze this breakthrough and present it to her when she is about seventeen and brings a boyfriend home for the first time.

Digestive upsets

Vomiting frequently occurs the first time fathers come into contact with their babies' stools. This can be frightening for a young baby so try to make it into a game or pull the neck of your sweater up over your mouth and nose. If you are wearing a V-neck or, worse still, a cardigan, try to distract the child by setting some furniture alight or smearing nappy-rash cream on the radiator.

Sleep

This is very unusual and not worth worrying about. It's only likely to happen if you are driving or operating heavy machinery.

Exercises

Babies and toddlers need to exercise. However, there is no need for them to start pumping iron unless you're the sort of father who wants to raise boys with an unhealthy interest in survival magazines and dog-breeding. Children get most of their exercise during energetic play. Studies have shown that, whereas mothers tend to play games which stimulate intellect and concentration, fathers engage in more lively, physical play. You'll have seen men with one-year-olds at parties saying, 'Come on, Myron, show everyone how you can somersault off my shoulders and land on your head.' Lifting, throwing and endangering children demonstrate a man's patriarchy to others, and it's a way of showing how much the child can do, if forced. Luckily, the kids seem to enjoy it and it teaches them, if nothing else, not to trust a grown-up's ability to catch.

Even very young babies benefit from gentle exercise. Responsible child-care books or your health visitor will show you safe and comfortable ways of exercising limbs. But don't expect much from newborns because they're crap, to be honest.

The best exercise, whether you're six months or sixty, is generally held to be swimming. Some parents are of the opinion that children have a natural ability to swim. My own father took it upon himself to introduce me to the Aldershot Lido before I was out of nappies. Unfortunately, the nappies filled with water and I sank. But his intuition was not without foundation. After a few seconds underwater, and once I had freed myself from my cot, that mysterious animal instinct took over in me and I began to fly south for the winter.

My father continued in his efforts to teach me to swim for a few years. My mother seemed not to be concerned that his lack of success might in part have resulted from the fact that he was completely unable to swim himself. I suppose that, because a dad is supposed to be in charge of the physical, it fell to *him* to hold my chin out of the water and say, 'Kick your legs.'

6 The Rest of Your Child's Life

Bringing up children is largely a matter of trial and error. Many men have five or six children before they start to get the hang of it.

Early one morning, I awoke to find a little hand tugging at my pyjamas. I realised I was masturbating in my sleep. But some years later when I was about to become a father, a very wise man gave me a piece of advice which I have found absolutely invaluable. You may not be so lucky. If there's no one giving you such pearls of wisdom, you'll just have to make it up as you go along.

Many years ago, I was sharing a joke with a comedian friend of mine. Material was hard to come by in those days and there weren't enough jokes to go round. But then my friend started to tell me about being a father. 'Jeremy,' he quipped, 'I tell you, become a father. You'll get so much new material out of the child.' Every morning, now, I sit my daughter down with a pen and paper, but so far her efforts have been absolute gibberish.

Nonetheless, if you are just embarking on the epic journey of fatherhood, there is much laughter ahead. Sometimes, my little one has had me in absolute fits, which I never suffered from before. But there have also been some very amusing moments, like the time when a popular TV personality was doing the horoscopes on breakfast television, and our little monkey, who can have been no more than eleven months old at the time, piped up, 'astronomer'. She meant, of course, 'astrologer'! Out of the mouths of babes, as they say!

There will, of course, be difficult and painful times too but, when you look back in years to come, you will be able to put them into proper perspective and also use them to illustrate the ingratitude of your children after all you've done for them.

Talking and listening

As well as talking to a child, it's vital that you listen to what you're saying, otherwise your mind will wander and you'll find you're talking bollocks. Think about what you're saying and why you're saying it, and ask yourself these questions:

1. What am I saying?
2. Why am I saying it?
3. What did you say? I wasn't listening.
4. Huh?

Sometimes when we think we're talking to children, we're not really *saying* anything to them. This is because they've left the room without our noticing. By not only talking but also using eye contact and physical closeness, we can achieve a greater awareness of when children have gone out. Then we can say dirty stuff without them hearing.

No matter how used we are to the colourful language we might hear in the pub or when we're driving alone, we tend to flinch when our kids let fly with a string of four-letter words. And no matter how careful we are around children, we can't control what they hear outside the home. Should we worry or is it pure hypocrisy to forbid the kind of language we use ourselves? Our motto here should be, 'Do as I say, not as I do.' So, when little Timothy tries out a new word – probably not even knowing what it means – take him aside and calmly say, 'You watch your fucking language in front of your mother.' That way, you've made it clear that there's a proper context for the use of particular words or phrases, and also involved your partner. Timothy will not hate you for setting clear parameters about what language is acceptable; he will blame his mother.

Has 'TV-itis' set in?

There is really no excuse for a child vegetating in front of violent and mindless cartoons on the television. There are plenty of films on video which a child can be sat in front of. By telling yourself, 'It's a classic' or 'The animation is far superior to the rubbish they do nowadays,' you can work through any damaging feelings of guilt you may have.

Some programmes are very educational and, using your video recorder, you can build up quite a TV encyclopaedia. There are some very informative series about nature, for example. Instead of seeing space monsters tearing each other to pieces, your child can learn about the way actual wild animals tear each other to pieces. And what looks like a soppy look-and-learn video about playful chimpanzees can be every bit as stomach-churning as the uncut version of *Deliverance*.

Sesame Street is a godsend to fathers. It is well-made, funny and educational, although Big Bird is a bit of a wanker. If your child won't watch it, tape it and watch it when she's asleep. Most kids love it, though. The repetition and pictorial reinforcement of numbers, letters, words and concepts over a long period is an excellent method of facilitating the assimilation of knowledge. So tape the show and keep playing it back all day. Your child will eventually wander off and get on with putting keys in the lavatory but if you stick with it you will reach an advanced transcendental state and greater enlightenment.

Books, toys and gender

Kids' books have moved on since I was young. When I was a boy, my reading consisted of books like *War and Killing for Boys*, *A Hundred Favourite Wars* and

Paddington Invades Vietnam. I was ten before I realised that Britain was no longer at war with Germany. I thought that the German language consisted of the expressions 'Aaaarrrggghhh, Himmel!' and 'Mein Gott, ze prisoners are escaping!'; and that 'Aaaiyeeeeeee!' was Japanese for 'Oh, I've been shot.'

Even though my parents discouraged war toys, the very language they used was informed by a culture of militarism. If I came home with a bruised shin or a grazed knee, my father would say, 'Been in the wars?' Apart from anything else, this was something of an overstatement; if I'd come home with one lung missing and a tank track across my face, dragging bits of barbed wire and writing poetry, the expression might have had some meaning.

All this was compounded by the fact that I grew up near to Aldershot, home of the British Army. At school fêtes, soldiers would give us displays and demonstrations of how to dismantle a railway carriage and transport it through a ticket barrier, how to put an amusement arcade out of action without the use of explosives and, of course, 'Unarmed Combat', which means shooting people who are unarmed.

It was deemed to be entirely appropriate that children, and particularly boys, should have it drummed into them that the answer to the world's problems was the British Army. Today's childhood heroes are much more likely to be individuals or small groups armed with chain-sticks and bamboo poles. This change is a consequence of the fact that you can't fit the Eighth Infantry onto a Game Boy. But the underlying message is still one of great violence. So how much does this affect children?

When the Teenage Mutant Ninja Turtles were first imported into this country from America, it was decided that they should be renamed the Teenage Mutant *Hero* Turtles. It was felt that the word 'Ninja' would be disturbing to young minds. The idea that there are six-foot talking reptiles living in the drains wasn't felt to be disturbing but the word 'Ninja' would turn our children into psychotic, bedwetting vigilantes. Oddly, they didn't change the word 'Mutant' to 'Well-built' or something like it. Mutation is acceptable subject matter for children's entertainment in a culture where we have changed the word 'Windscale' to 'Sellafield'. I suspect that the real objection to the word 'Ninja' was that it's foreign.

But it is often argued that parents, particularly fathers, condition boys into aggression and girls into domesticity. Look at yourself as a man, think about your own upbringing, and ask yourself these questions:

1. Am I aggressive?
2. Who's asking?
3. Me, want to make something of it?
4. You and whose army?

Some believe that, regardless of conditioning, boys are innately more aggressive than girls. Dr Bernard O'White of Harvard argues that male and female hormones produce different behaviour patterns:

> One cannot bend nature. However much liberal theorists play down the differences between the sexes, our bodies tell us different. All human activity is triggered by chemical impulses and these in turn are governed by hormones. It is a woman's oestrogen that makes her buy a dress, put on make-up or have a gossip with the gals, just as it controls her reproductive cycle. A woman takes to child-rearing just as surely as a bird knows how to fly. Likewise, a man is a product of his testosterone. Whether he's putting up shelves, fixing stuff or punching someone's lights out, he's doing what a man has to do, with God on his side. No son of mine ever dodged the draft. I'm proud to be an Okie from Muskogee. God bless America.[1]

It seems likely, however, that, if we surround boys with images of combat and girls with images of passivity, it will affect the way they think, and that a man's preconception of how his children are ordained to

[1] David Duke Memorial Lecture, 1991

behave will influence how he treats them. Many fathers think that a boy mustn't be given a doll to play with, because it will turn him into an effeminate homosexual, although if a *man* plays with a rubber replica of a woman, he is generally considered to be a heterosexual, albeit not a happy one.

The toy doll will usually be given to the daughter, to whom the father will also speak more tenderly. She will be 'Daddy's little princess' – as if comparison with an educationally-subnormal member of the ruling class is in some way a compliment. Some people think the reason for male homosexuality is that boys are treated *too* tenderly. The real reason is more likely to be that someone has to buy Barbra Streisand records.[1]

In most cases, however, we don't so much want to mould our children by what they play with or read, we simply think it's what they'll like, or what will enable them to fit in with their peers. This brings us onto the question of other children.

Other children

Children can be very cruel. Every classroom seems to be a hierarchy with bullies at the top and scapegoats at the bottom. When I was at primary school, our bully was called Guido. If you've ever wondered why slugs have no legs, it's because they were pulled off by children like Guido. He was fat, weak, stupid and cowardly but for some reason we accepted him as our bully. If we'd thought about it, he'd have made an excellent scapegoat.

Traditionally, fathers have been divided between those who want a child to stand up for himself and those who think that whatever trouble happens at school is the child's fault. Some kids were brought up always to

[1] There seems to be less concern that girls may turn out to be lesbians. Most men never give much thought to lesbianism, except in their sexual fantasies.

fight back, whether or not they had haemophilia. Others would go home bound, gagged and on fire to a father who would say, 'What have I told you about fighting?' The child would be told to turn the other cheek in future, even though it was stapled to a blackboard.

An alternative to these extremes is to teach the child to be popular by impersonating schoolteachers, so that his wit and personality are his defence mechanisms and he can become a stand-up comedian. The problem here is that, when comedians say in interviews that this is how they got into comedy, it is usually not true. They say it because they are very dull off-stage and can't think of anything else to say.

If your child is being picked on, or indeed is picking on others, the best thing to do is meet with the other kids' dads, form a men's group, and organise a rota whereby all the kids get a turn both at being picked on and at bullying.

Is there such a thing as a bad child?

Christians use baptism to cleanse away original sin, although christening normally takes place when the worst thing a person's ever done is keep her parents awake all night. The conservative view of humanity is that we are wild animals until broken, tamed and socialised. We might be tempted to believe this when we witness the behaviour of children whose parents don't believe in saying 'no'.

'Sophie, I want you to look at why you think it is that something positive will be generated by you doing that,' says Malcolm, as Sophie stands on the dinner table urinating into the salad.

But is the child undisciplined or simply commenting on the nightmare of having macrobiotic parents? Part of us thinks, 'That child's been allowed to run riot for too long' or even, 'That child needs a good smack,' while part of us thinks, 'Go for it, Sophie!'

On the other hand, we've all seen children sustaining

head injuries from parents who seem to think dishing them out is a natural part of shopping. 'Violence breeds violence,' we mutter to ourselves, feeling we'd be meddling if we gave vent to, 'Why don't you leave him alone, you fucking bastard?' Then there are the middle-class parents who are quite happy for little Louisa to kill or maim other toddlers in the park because the insurance will cover it. So what's the answer? I don't know.

A favourite way of putting a child off smoking cigarettes is to let them smoke a whole packet. We could apply this principle to all misbehaviour. Maybe that's why Louisa has free rein. And perhaps once a child has destroyed your whole house, she might get sick of it and help you build a new one. Or she may get a taste for it and be getting through twenty houses a day by the time she's eleven. The easiest thing to do in this context is to put everything out of the child's reach – you may decide to move to a third floor flat and rent the child one on the ground floor.

Confusion in the signals children get from us may arise because we operate different standards in our own homes from the ones we apply in someone else's. You may feel that children should be 'on their best behaviour' when they're out. However, disciplining children in front of others is embarrassing for you and humiliating for them so it's best to draw a clear distinction between your stuff and other people's. People shouldn't have you over if they don't want their things trashed. Of course, I sympathise with people who are trying to have a quiet meal out and are disturbed by noisy brats banging on the table and getting food everywhere, but they shouldn't go to Mexican restaurants if they don't want to be surrounded by advertising executives.

What should we tell our kids?

We don't want to indoctrinate our children. We also don't want to scare them. On the other hand, we don't want to delude them. But we've got to tell them something.

You've probably got certain values and principles which you want your kids to grow up with. You may, for example, be concerned about protecting the environment. In this case, you should keep kids away from it as much as possible.

But your child will probably question you about things before you've even thought of broaching the issue with her. When she says, 'Daddy, why don't you and Mummy like Mr Major?' you can't very well say, 'Because he's a Tory bastard'; she won't know what a Tory is. You must try to relate ideas to things she knows about. So, if she asks you why you don't like Mr Major, you might reply, 'Well, we don't all like everything. You don't like sprouts or liver do you? Well, Mr Major wants to make you eat them every day for the rest of your life.'

You will probably find that your child is captivated by royalty because of its fairy-tale imagery. Every other children's story is about kings and princesses. You may, as we have seen, use the terminology yourself. If you are of the opinion that the Queen is God's representative on Earth, there is so much subliminal indoctrination to support your view, that you'll never even have to tackle the subject. If, on the other hand, you think the monarchy are the living icons of a system that is rotten to its foundations, you may want to counterbalance the royalist propaganda surrounding your child by offering another perspective. An excellent educational toy is the Playfolk French Revolution set with the detachable heads.

Religion is a tricky one. If you have a devout faith, you will want your child to share it. You may also worry that, without its guiding light, the child will fall prey to other temptations. When I was ten, I got mixed up with a sinister, phoney religious cult – my parents took me to church. Fortunately, the Church of England isn't the kind of denomination to screw up your life, which also means it's no fun and its appeal tarnishes quite quickly.

I have to say that, if a religion needs children to be brought up in it, it must have a problem convincing adults. On the other hand, many children draw some comfort from the idea of a God. When I was quite young, our family dog died and I was told by my father that she had 'gone to live with Jesus'. For years I thought Jesus must, therefore, live under our compost heap. But was my father wrong? Would it have been better to say, 'She's dead, dead, like Great Gran, Santa and the Age of Steam'?

Only you can decide whether you think you are brainwashing or being dishonest to a child. 'The Truth' is unbearable for most adults so it's probably not fair to expect a four-year-old to take it on board. On the other hand, you've got to do something to prepare them for the downward spiral of disappointment and despair that is human existence. The best thing is to find a happy medium.

When it comes to beliefs, you may want to approach them like this:

'Some people believe that there is a God. Personally, I don't, but that's not to say that I'm right necessarily.'

The problem here is that you have now established to your child the possibility that you are fallible. When you try to put her to bed that night, she will say:

'Although you have every right to your opinion that it's my bedtime, I myself am of the view that it's too early, and that's a matter for my conscience alone. I suppose we must just agree to differ.'

Then you'll have to explain to her the arguments for and against proportional representation, and she'll fall asleep anyway.

Education

On balance, this is probably a good idea, if only to get the child out of the house once in a while. But you must see your child's education as a partnership involving the school, the child and you. Nowadays, parents are much more involved in the education of their children because they have to buy everything for the schools.

You may decide to take on the job of educating a child yourself. Fathers who believe their children to be prodigies often choose to keep them at home until they go to university, to prevent their being held back by children who are well-adjusted or happy.

You may feel that you want to send your children away to boarding schools if, for some reason, you don't like them. A word of warning, however – although private education teaches people to think they're entitled to own and run everything, it can be very expensive and may cost even more than sending kids to the local state school.

In this chapter, we have covered all the problems you are likely to face as a father apart from illness, drugs, divorce, disability, the inner torment of teenagers, the torment of bringing up teenagers, kids leaving home and being unemployed in a world with no clean air or water, where all the nice art-deco cinemas have been knocked down and where there will never be another Labour government, worrying about your kids for the rest of your life, and them despising you and not wanting you to live with them when you're old.

In the next part of the book, we shall look at fatherhood from a cultural and historical perspective maybe.

Further reading: Your children's diaries

Part Two

Fatherhood From a Cultural and Historical Perspective Maybe

7 God the Father

The father of all humanity is of course God. He is also the father of Jesus, who was the son of Mary who, rather confusingly, is the Mother of God.

There are divergent theological explanations for all this. The most popular interpretation is that God and Jesus, as well as being father and son, were the same person, which is how we know that God had long hair and a beard. Jesus is God and God is Jesus. After all, we never see them in the same room, except after the ascension when Jesus 'sat on the right hand of God' (Mark 16:19). This expression seems peculiar to us today and conjures up a rather bizarre image, but the meaning is made clearer by the contemporary language of the 1983 *Modern Revised Contemporary Newish English Bible-Type Book*. The phrase becomes, 'Jesus was a glove puppet.' There is now considerable archaeological evidence to suggest that God created a puppet which came to life. This interpretation would seem to support claims that the New Testament story is a version of a much earlier pagan myth, that of Pinocchio. Indeed, if one counts the letters in God's name and adds the number of Gospels the total is seven, almost the same number of letters as in Geppetto, Pinocchio's father (see *Chapter Nine*).

Much of the problem with understanding the Bible is making sense of the language. For example, the 'begetting' which takes place in the Old Testament is preceded by men 'knowing' their wives, i.e. knowledge means sex. This linguistic key provides a whole new connotation to the phrase 'nodding acquaintance'.

The Creation

With these basic analytical tools at our disposal, let's start at the Beginning. God creates Adam, fully grown up. This cuts out any real parenting by God and it is really Adam who is the first father. Eve bears him two sons, Cain and Abel. Cain kills Abel and is banished. I should say at this point that the way to confront sibling rivalry is always to try and involve the older child in the new arrival and not let him feel unwanted and resentful. Having let the situation get out of hand, Adam's only option was probably to punish Cain's behaviour, although banishment is very long-term and should really only be used as a last resort.

This sequence of events leaves Adam and Eve effectively childless. By the time Eve conceives their third child Seth, they are one hundred and thirty years old. Late pregnancies like this are very common in the Old Testament and should give encouragement to older couples. It is important, however, that both parents are in very good health. Genesis 5:26 tells us, 'And the Lord said unto Adam, Be careful not to bend as you collapse the buggy.' (*Authorised Version*, 1611)

Abraham and Isaac

This is perhaps the best-known father/child relationship in the Old Testament. The story most commonly associated with Abraham and Isaac gives us a perfect example of God's attitude to his earthly children, and also his effect upon men as fathers. The key word is Faith.

One day, Abraham is in the Middle East doing general biblical things. He is now several hundred years old and probably telling some stranger that every other face in the post office is black nowadays. God speaks to Abraham:

'Abraham, are you doing anything at the moment?'
'Nothing special, why?'

'Well, it's about your son Isaac.'

'He's not in any trouble is he?'

'No, no; nothing like that. It's just that I want you to take him up to the top of a mountain, stab him to death and burn him as a sacrifice to me.'

'Oh.'

'Well, you don't sound very pleased. Don't you want to?'

'Oh, it's not that. It's just that I promised to take him to the football this afternoon.'

'All right, well, tomorrow then.'

'Okay, thanks, God.'

So, bright and early next morning, Abraham sets off with Isaac and a load of firewood to the land of Moria, where God shows him the mountain he has chosen. They climb. Isaac is curious.

'Golly, Dad, that's a lot of kindling. What are we sacrificing?'

'Oh, er, just a few sausages, couple of chops.'

'Don't we need a lamb or something for a sacrifice?'

'Er, yes, the Lord will provide us with a lamb in due course.'

'Oh, why are you tying me to this altar? Is it a game?'

'That's right, Isaac, a game. Keep still, there's a good lad . . . Now you might feel a violent stabbing sensation.'

At this moment, the Angel of the Lord calls to him.

'Abraham! What the hell are you doing?'

'I'm killing him, aren't I? It was God's idea, not mine.'

'Abraham, it was a test. A test of faith. You shouldn't take God so literally all the time. He doesn't really want you to kill Isaac. He's not a complete sod, you know.'

So Abraham doesn't kill Isaac. Instead he sacrifices a ram which has miraculously appeared in a thicket. This is all very well for him, but what about Isaac? Abraham had reconciled himself to the idea of a dead son. He's now got a son who's completely alive and knows that Dad is quite prepared to murder him in cold blood when asked to do so. One would imagine a rather frosty atmosphere as the two prepare to go all the way down the mountain together. Isaac was probably extremely reluctant to go first.

The New Testament

How much, then, does our heavenly Father love us? Well, apparently, God so loved the world that he gave us his only begotten son. Let us pause to think about that. God loved the world so much, he didn't come himself; he sent his little boy. Maybe for an Oscar nomination he would show up in person, but for the salvation of humankind, he delegates.

If Abraham's concept of parental responsibility seems lacking, God's was a disaster. Right from the word 'Go', there is a marked lack of closeness between God and Jesus. It is one thing for a man not to be present at the birth of his child, but to be absent from the conception is unforgivable. It's left to the Angel Gabriel to deliver the tidings to the Virgin Mary. If a woman opts for artificial insemination by donor, she accepts that, to some extent, she has chosen to take pot luck. But to be told by a Christmas-tree decoration that one will shortly be up the stick courtesy of a third party is something of a bombshell (Luke 1:30–31, *Authorised Version*).

Mary is no expert on fertility but it is clear even to her that something would appear to be missing from the equation. The explanation afforded by Gabriel is that 'The Holy Ghost shall come upon thee' (Luke 1:35). Again, the Scriptures leave us with a rather unpleasant picture in our minds. And how, one wonders, is Mary supposed to break the news to Joseph, a devoted husband with a successful carpentry business and normal sperm count? Fortunately, the Angel of the Lord backs up her story and Joseph shows considerable forbearance as they set off to Bethlehem to pay his taxes. On the plus side, if the baby comes in time, his personal allowance will go up. Nonetheless, in my

The Annunciation by Duccio.
Note Angel of the Lord's obscene gesture.

Joseph Denies It's His by van Eyck

opinion, Christian worshippers pay scant regard to the man who brought God's son up as his own. He is constantly marginalised by the adoration of the Blessed Virgin. On the other hand, she does deliver a baby with a circle of wire poking out of the back of his head, and there were no epidurals in those days.

Assuming, as the Christian faith does, that God intends his son to be the Messiah, he sends him into the world with a number of disadvantages. Firstly, of all the names he could have chosen for him, God picks an expletive. True, Jesus Christ is better than Jesus Wept or Suffering Christ. But one can't envy our Lord's second coming if there's a chance he's going to be called Bollocks or Fuck My Old Boots.

Secondly, if Jesus is supposed to be the King of the Jews, why does he look like Robert Powell? Perhaps God fears that, if his son looks too Jewish, he'll never get into movies.

To be fair, God does produce a son who is unusually gifted. Jesus makes the lame walk, for example. But so do British Rail. On the miracle front, I find the prophet Moses much more impressive. How many new-born babies have you come across who can navigate a wicker basket through a load of bulrushes? Most of Jesus's miracles would indicate that he missed his vocation and should have been in catering.

But one has to feel a certain sympathy for Jesus. His role on Earth is to save humanity by getting them to repent for their sins. This they signally fail to do, so Jesus is punished for all the sins of all of humankind everywhere in history ever. This seems rather harsh. It's an extreme way for God to prove he doesn't believe in nepotism. In the Old Testament, God's approach to bringing humans into line is starkly different. By and large, he does his own dirty work. He has angels as henchmen and messengers but, when it comes to laying down the law, he knows who his enemies are and his retribution is terrible. He wipes out Sodom and Gomorrah; he kills the firstborn; there are plagues of locusts and frogs and rivers running blood; the entire Egyptian army is drowned. But come the New Testament it's a question of 'Repent or the kid gets it.'

Of course, Jesus does get it. One is left asking, why, when Jesus is most in need of a miracle, does he not use one? One flash of the old magic would have shut up all the scribes and Pharisees, proved he was the Son of God, got one-up on Barabbas, won Pilate over and got himself out of extremely hot water.

It may be that it's hard to do a miracle when one is tense; it's probably got a lot to do with breathing and relaxation, although I'm guessing at this point. Or perhaps he was just tired of doing miracles, always being expected to knock one off at the drop of a hat. I suspect that, if Mary and Joseph were aware of his abilities when he was younger, the precocious Jesus must often have found himself the focus of unwanted attention at family gatherings:

'Come along, Jesus, do one of your miracles for the guests.'

'Oh, Dad, I don't want to.'

'Come along, Auntie Ruth hasn't seen your Water-into-Wine.'

'Oh Dad, can't I go to the temple?'

'No, you can't go to the temple!'

'You're not my real dad! God's my real dad.'

'I think you'd better go straight upstairs, young man! And tidy your room – it's full of lepers.'

But perhaps the real reason Jesus put up so little resistance in the face of his persecutors was his faith in his father. He simply couldn't believe that the old man would let him down quite so badly. He didn't think there was actually going to be a crucifixion. He thought there'd be a big rescue number at the end of the movie, with angels in balaclavas hurling stun grenades and God abseiling down from a cloud.

No such fatherly interest was forthcoming and the crucifixion went ahead. Initially, Jesus was fairly chipper about the situation. But after a while, he had

what we call his 'moment of doubt', which is fair
enough; by this stage he'd got grounds for wondering if
the whole plan wasn't going horribly wrong. He must
have thought, 'I'm the Messiah; I'm the King of the
Jews; I'm the Prince of Peace; I'm the Son of God . . . I'm
nailed to a piece of wood.' Finally, rather late in the day,
he cried out for attention from his father, 'My God! My
God! Why hast thou forsaken me?' But only according to
Matthew and Mark. According to Luke, he shouted,
'Father, unto thy hands I commend my spirit,' which is
a totally different version of events, but that's journal-
ism for you. According to the police, he beat himself up
and made a full confession.

Whatever Jesus shouted, God, at last, responded, 'Oh,
sorry son, I wasn't listening. What was that?' But it was
too late. Jesus had given up the ghost.

How could a father have become so remote from his
child? To start with, God had a son for all the wrong
reasons. He was more concerned to impress others than
to be a father to his son. He showed no real interest in
his son's development but placed unreasonable expecta-
tions on him. There was no positive encouragement,
only the threat of punishment. When Jesus did not fulfil
these hopes, the punishment was severe.

And what of us, God's earthly children? I am sure we
are also a great disappointment to him but there is such
a lack of communication that it's hard to know what's
on his mind. Many claim to hear messages from him but
the trouble is that large numbers of people also say that
Elvis tells them what the weather's going to be. James
Anderton, the former Chief Constable of Greater Man-
chester, once said that God was speaking through him.
It's quite possible – I'm sure that even God talks out of
his arse sometimes. Anderton's pronouncements
claimed, among other things, that Aids was sent by God
to punish people for being homosexual. What, then, was
the Black Death for? To punish people for wearing
period costume?

Others have seen moving statues and weeping

Madonnas. If God is trying to tell us something, it's certainly not clear what it is. Maybe these are signs that the Son of God is coming again. The Son of God may have other ideas.

Lest this chapter be considered blasphemous, I should make my own relationship with our Father quite clear: I don't believe in him and he doesn't answer my prayers.

8 'Hi, Kids, I'm Home!'

Men who wish to become sitcom fathers must bear in mind certain preconditions.

Firstly, it is essential that you own a home which is much bigger than your income can possibly support. TV sitcom homes are extremely large, partly because they need to accommodate several cameras and an audience of two to three hundred people. It is also important that your house is built using materials that vibrate a lot.

Secondly, you must not discuss your job with your family. This is not because it has anything to do with national security. Rather, it is a non-specific sort of job – preferably white-collar – with flexible hours allowing you to come home unexpectedly for plot reasons or simply be at home all of the time. It is sufficient for your children to know that work makes you very tired, so that you can emphasise all the sacrifices you've made for them which they don't appreciate.

They may be as old as thirty but will either live with you or visit you constantly without warning. You will never visit their homes and, to all intents and purposes, their homes do not exist.

As society has changed, making children more central to their fathers' lives, the reverse has happened in British situation comedy. Gone are the days when one might see a show called *Dear Daddy* or *Glory be to the Father*, in which the main character's sole trait was that he had children. But a move back to child-centred comedy will inevitably happen in the nineties, as British television catches up with America.

Where fatherhood *is* central or more than incidental to a sitcom, the overriding feature of the father's role is a hangdog and resigned disapproval of his children's lifestyles. A daughter will have an unsavoury boyfriend and a son will have left-wing political connections and/ or teeshirts. If, on the other hand, you are a radical veteran of the sixties, your disappointing children will be in the Young Conservatives and invite former SS officers to the house when your men's group is meeting in the living-room.

You will also have to contend with the fact that your offspring are prey to bizarre fashions, all of which are many years out of date. Here is a typical scenario:

> **Jenny** *enters in New Romantic gear.*
> **Dad**   What on earth do you look like?
> *Audience laughter.*
> **Jenny**   All the kids at college are wearing this, Dad.
> **Dad**   Good grief! School was bad enough: earrings, drainpipe trousers, Mohican hairstyles . . . and that was just the teachers!
> *Audience laughter.*
> **Jenny**   Oh, Daddy, you're so set in your ways!
> **Dad**   I'll have you know your mother and I were the toast of Frinton-on-Sea in 1962. And where's that idle layabout of a brother of yours? Still in bed I suppose. Why your ex-stepmother married him I'll never know.
> *Enter* **Tom** *in pyjamas, hair tousled, and* **Julie**, *immaculately dressed.*
> **Dad**   Talk of the devil!
> **Tom**   Hi, Dad. Wicked. Er, this is Julie.
> **Julie**   Hi.
> **Dad**   What happened to Natalie?
> **Tom**   We got divorced yesterday, didn't I say? I met Julie in court.

Julie   Your son kindly offered to help me with my briefs.
Dad   I'll bet!
Audience laughter.

Expectant British sitcom fathers need not feel daunted. Their parental responsibilities will involve no more than this kind of upbraiding banter. So have fun! And DON'T PANIC!

American sitcom fathers

So far we have looked at male parenting in UK sitcom. The vast majority of sitcom fathers, however, are American. If you are in this category, you may have young children. British children cannot act, so a British sitcom father's family are grown up. They cannot act either but at least they can stand under studio lights without getting hot and bothered and sometimes don't burst into tears when shouted at by a director.

In the United States, sitcom dads not only have younger children but they also have more of them. You may have forty or fifty children spanning a large age range. Some may be older than you and of widely divergent racial origins, although there is no suggestion that they are not your natural children except in cases where they are from other galaxies or periods of history.

You may have only one child, and she may have several other fathers in addition to you, all of whom happen to be your flatmates. In this situation, there is no way of determining which of you is the natural father as there are no blood tests in sitcom and the child won't look remotely like any of you.

As a US sitcom dad, you will be under a lot more stress than your British counterparts. Your life will revolve almost entirely around your children. Not only are you likely to have more and younger children, but they will be unnervingly articulate and able to construct quite elaborate jokes and time them correctly, as well as having a flair for enacting complete song-and-dance routines from Broadway musicals.

The fact that your kids are uncommonly gifted means that you will need to devote a lot of one-on-one time to each of them, for periods of twenty to twenty-five minutes, allowing for advertising. Fortunately, while you are focusing your concentration on one child, the others will generally be quite content not to be the centre of attention. They will happily make themselves scarce – sometimes for several episodes at a time if they get a film part. American children can also drive from the age of six and, if the stairs are near the front door, one of them can make a token appearance, borrow the car and leave the house without interrupting the main father/child interaction. It is vital that this discussion takes centre-stage and is undisturbed, so that your sitcom child feels comfortable with a level of communication with you which is quite impossible between an adult and a normal child.

Your sitcom child will try to hide things from you. There are several tell-tale signs of this, both from the child, who will display a furtive awkwardness, and from your partner, who will say, 'Do you think Billy's hiding something from us?'

Whatever Billy is hiding, it will place him in a moral dilemma, the resolution of which will bring him one step closer to adulthood. He will not be hiding anything as simple as solo acts of depravity performed while in the bathroom for extended periods. It is more likely to involve dishonesty, small-scale theft, reckless skateboarding, the company of children who are a bad influence, showing off or mild drug abuse.

Lying is nothing to worry about. Billy is simply protecting a classmate by covering up for him, either because of intimidation or because the child's father is unemployed and dying of leprosy. Billy has forgotten that, no matter how much we sympathise with the unfortunate, stealing candy is still a crime. It doesn't matter whether the other child *does* get sent away to a special school or his parents do starve, right is right and wrong is wrong. You must impress upon your child that every person can be what he wants to be. The fact that this is untrue should not discourage you. Remember, the audience is there to support you, and when Billy does come round to your way of thinking, they will give you a warm round of applause and shouts of 'Yeah', because they think it's real life.

The best way to show Billy what he must do is to use personal reminiscence and analogy, as in this example:

Dad   Billy, I used to be a kid once, just like you. Oh, it's hard to believe, I know, but I was. I remember one time I found myself in a situation a whole lot like the one you're in now.

Billy   What did you do, Daddy?

Dad   I did the right thing, Billy.

Billy   And you think I thould do the right thing too?

Dad   Only you can answer that question, Billy.

Billy   Thanks, Daddy.

All forms of unacceptable behaviour should be approached in this way. In rare cases, a sitcom child may use intravenous drugs or join a fundamentalist or diabolist group, but it's important to recognise that this is only a bid for attention. It may well be that, while you are devoting so much time to your better-scripted children, a child who is not so well fleshed out gets neglected. He therefore needs to identify himself as a character and if this means flirting with Satanism so be it. Once he's asserted himself, the plot device will simply disappear and next week he'll be into something else.

If, however, your children start trying to assert themselves as being *distinct* from the family group, rather than included in it, you must illustrate to them that the way to do this is through competitive sporting achievements and capitalist enterprise. Individual exploits like becoming a successful drag queen should never endanger the cohesion of the family unit. However suffocating the nuclear family may be, it is the foundation stone not only of our whole way of life but of sitcom itself.

So much for the small screen. In the next chapter we go to the movies.

9 Night of the Living Dad: Fathers on Film

Today's movie fathers are a million miles away from the over-dramatised, patriarchal bullies of the silent era. They are less convincing for a start. But one thing remains the same: the Hollywood dad has a couple of hours in which to make the transition from young romantic lead to older character actor. That is why the best movie father was Spencer Tracy who was born old.

As a movie father, you will initially have difficulty in relating to your children, and not only because they are odious little stage-school bastards. By the end of the film, you will have developed a much closer empathy and rapport with them and also made a mental note never to work with children again. Let us take *Meet Me in St Louis*. In this powerful musical Alonzo Smith (Leon Ames) wants to uproot his family and attempt to build a future in New York. In a disturbing and controversial scene during which the young Margaret O'Brien decapitates several snowmen, Smith is jolted into an understanding of how he has put his career before the emotional needs of his children. Where the film falls down is that the audience is forced to recognise its own desire to decapitate Margaret O'Brien.

There are similarities here with *Mary Poppins*. In both films, the first appearance of the stiff-necked Edwardian father is his return home from work with the expectation that his domestic and familial regime will simply fall into place around him. And most people would also like to decapitate Julie Andrews.

The character of the chimney sweep in *Mary Poppins*,

played by Dick Van Dyke, is crucial in making David Tomlinson realise that it is he, the father, who is really missing out in his relationship with his children. He argues that men effectively lose their children by never really knowing them.

But Van Dyke's plea leaves us with a problem that needs to be addressed. The question is: what the fuck does he think that accent sounds like? Who told him that cockneys sound like that and why did the farm animals in the animated hallucination scene – which, incidentally, would have benefitted from a bit of Steppenwolf and Denis Hopper playing one of the penguins – take a lead from Dick Van Dyke? They didn't even have to be cockneys; there are hardly any East London farm animals apart from a few goats on city farms – and they're middle class.

Anyway, the point is that in most films it is the father and not the children who must learn a lesson about life. In Sidney Lumet's classic jury-room drama *Twelve Angry Men*, the Lee J. Cobb character has to face up to the fact that the breakdown of his relationship with his own son makes him want to believe that the accused is guilty of murdering his father. In *The Little Mermaid* King Triton realises that his daughter Ariel's love for a human prince cannot be overruled, and he turns her tail into legs, so that the couple can have sex normally and Prince Eric does not have to ejaculate onto mermaid's roe at the bottom of the sea.

If you are about to become a father in a movie, learn from the mistakes of your predecessors, especially if, like Pinocchio's father, you are making your own child. Geppetto takes no account of the fact that a wooden boy has special needs. He has barely finished sanding him down when he wishes on a star that Pinocchio were a real boy. Although there is no vetting procedure for such an application, the Blue Fairy who brings Pinocchio to life clearly states that the request for him to become 'real' will have to await consideration, pending his ability to prove himself brave, truthful and unselfish, in accordance with the Bravery, Truth and Unselfishness clauses of the 1936 Adoption Act.

In spite of the fact that Pinocchio is patently still wooden, Geppetto packs him straight off to school the next morning, with no apparent thought for the consequences. The overwhelming likelihood is that he will be well behind the other children, functionally illiterate and unused to structured learning. One has a right to expect that fathers of marionettes, with or without strings, will make a preparatory trip to a new school, meet the teachers and make an assessment of whether the school has adequate resources for ligneous children. The teachers must allow for the fact that the child is likely to come up against considerable prejudice from non-puppet children. Parents should also be aware that a newly-carved child has no experience or point of reference. He is easy prey for any unscrupulous charlatan promising a successful career in the theatre. Tell the child, 'If someone you don't know approaches you and sings, "Hi-diddle-di-dee, an actor's life for me", just say "no".'

Pinocchio is at least more fortunate than Dumbo, who has no idea who his father is, nor indeed, given that he was a stork delivery, whether or not he has one. One assumes that he hasn't. If he has, there must be another elephant somewhere with ears that size and you'd think he'd have the decency not to have children.

Likewise, Satan in *Rosemary's Baby* leaves a son with abnormally bloodshot eyes to grow up with a normal mother. The Devil has fathered more than one child in the cinema.[1] All of the Antichrist's children have had enormous difficulty in being assimilated, even though some of them are superficially like any other child, apart from having 666 written behind their ears in biro.

---

[1] When I say 'in the cinema', I mean, in films, not literally in the cinema; Satan is like God in that he can make a woman pregnant without going to the pictures with her.

There are some exemplary film fathers, like Atticus in *To Kill a Mockingbird* or Pongo in *A Hundred and One Dalmatians*. At the other end of the spectrum, there are the hopeless cases like Cal's father in *East of Eden* and Jim Dear in *Lady and the Tramp*, who leaves his young baby with Aunt Sarah, a wholly inappropriate babysitter with Siamese cats. Clearly, neither man has bonded properly. This problem crops up time and time again. Bambi has a father who is really not there for him. Darth Vader does not even tell Luke Skywalker that they are father and son until shortly before he cuts off his hand with a light-sabre.

There may be cases when, as a movie father, you can't help being remote from your children. This may not just be because your scenes are shot on different days. King Stefan in *Sleeping Beauty* has to let the three good fairies foster his daughter until her sixteenth birthday because she is at risk from spinning wheels. The father of *The Railway Children*, absent for most of the film, is serving a sentence for a crime he did not commit. If you are a real-life father who is wrongly convicted, you can expect to spend a couple of decades trying to convince people that you were fitted up by the police. Luckily, in a British family film like *The Railway Children*, your children just have to ask the kindly old gentleman who owns the railway company to make a few enquiries, and you will be released immediately. Moreover, real-life characters like Lord Lane are far too disturbing ever to make it onto the silver screen.

Of course, a movie father usually begins as a father in a play or a book. Being a father in a play is the same as being a father in a film except that you have to shout so people can hear you. A good choice of author is Tennessee Williams who wrote in a lot of shouting. One of the reasons for all the shouting in Williams's work was that the characters were full of despair about the future, knowing that they would lose their jobs to more bankable stars when the play became a movie.

Williams's most famous father was Big Daddy in *Cat*

on a Hot Tin Roof. Burl Ives was allowed to keep the part when it became a film, on condition that at no time during shooting would he break into 'The Ugly Bug Ball'.[1] Big Daddy has two sons. The younger is Brick, an alcoholic ex-footballer played by Paul Newman. Brick is his father's favourite son. This would seem to date from birth because, although Brick is a stupid name, it's not as stupid as Gooper, which is what he called the other one.

Many of Shakespeare's fathers have also transferred to films. Most find the move traumatic and have difficulty in adjusting to their reduced roles. Some, like Montagu and Capulet from *Romeo and Juliet* found themselves totally eclipsed and replaced by teenage street gangs called the Sharks and the Jets when their story became the Hollywood musical, *Seven Dwarfs for Seven Samurai.* But one Shakespearian father for whom the change from stage to screen has been beneficial is the ghost of Hamlet's father, because special effects are crap in the theatre and it always looks a bit daft to have some old lovey covered in talcum powder wander about the stage trying to look ethereal.

To finish on a positive note, there are some movie dads who can't do enough for their children, and the best of these is Marlon Brando in *The Godfather.* Most people's abiding memory of the film is the heart-warming way in which Don Corleone cultivates one of his godsons' interest in music. The band-leader who won't employ the boy wakes up one morning to find a horse's head next to him in bed. Of course, Sarah Brightman put up with that for several years, but in 1971, when the *The Godfather* was released and Andrew Lloyd Webber was relatively unknown, it was considered quite shocking. What's important is that Don Corleone realises that not all children are cut out to

---

[1] This was not likely as at that time he had not made *Summer Magic* which came out five years later.

follow in their godfathers' footsteps but that they may have other talents which need to be nurtured.

The Godfather marks the beginnings of the kind of father we now call New Man. In the next chapter we shall chart the sociological development of the institution of fatherhood in the twentieth century. Blimey.

10 From 'Sir' to 'Keith'

The institution of fatherhood in Britain has undergone a transformation in the twentieth century. In 1900, the only parenting a man did was to stand with his back to a fireplace saying, 'So, you want to marry my daughter,' even if he only had sons. But, as we saw in our discussion of *Mary Poppins*, the early part of the century witnessed the beginnings of the transition to a modern epoch in which men cry even more than their children.

A walk around a card shop will bear witness to the number of male models who are now prepared to be photographed in tender poses with young infants. It should be stressed, however, that these muscle-bound Adonises are not the real fathers of the children. No one with a new baby has the energy to pump iron for two hours a day. Moreover, you should never hold a naked baby boy up in front of you because he will urinate in your face.

Nonetheless, a social revolution has taken place. Men not only want to take more of a role in parenting, it is accepted that they should. Child-care books have made a radical departure since the days when the sole emphasis was on motherhood. Dr Belinda Ayckbourn in *The Complete Mother, Baby and Passing Reference to Father Book* advises men as follows:

> Today's father takes a much more active interest in child-care. You will obviously want to go straight back to work immediately after the birth but you may wish to pop back later on to see if your partner needs anything and if the baby's out of danger. You will, of course, have asked your mother to come and live with you for the first

six months, so you'll need to make up a bed in the living-room for yourself and your partner. Your partner will be very tired after all she's been through so you might offer her a lift home from the hospital. She may also have difficulty in juggling her domestic responsibilities with her new child-caring role for the first couple of days, so you could help out around the home by inviting her mother to stay as well.

So what happened to usher in this new era for fathers in the twentieth century? Historically, the nuclear family is quite a recent phenomenon. In pre-industrial Britain, most of the population lived quite communally. Luckily, they were also illiterate and couldn't leave terse notes to each other about whose turn it was to buy toilet paper. Fathers and mothers both worked the land and it was left to grandparents to stitch the children into hessian sacks and bury them in clay pits until they were fourteen.

The start of the Industrial Revolution was signalled by the discovery of penicillin by Spinning Jenny, the inventor of steam. Progressively, the largely rural population was driven off the land by rambling societies and began to settle in new towns like Harlow and Telford. From this time on, children didn't need to be babysat because they had jobs.

It wasn't until the nineteenth century that child labour began to be abolished. Opposition to reform was fierce. In 1837, the Royal Commission of Enquiry into Radicals Who Would Impede the Proper Labours of Journeymen Infants in the Soot-Mining Industry reported as follows:

These busybodies would impose by means of statute a maximum working week of but seventy-two hours for children being less than four years of age, and forbid that they be justly maimed in their pursuit of rightful toil. Such radicals hamper the liberty of those men who create the riches of our land. For that Britannia may remain the first among God's nations, and that she may long continue the slaughter of the heathen Arab to secure the passage of exotic oils from the East, the cost to manufacture must be low. Else, we should see the Prussian and the Frenchy surpass us in trade of chattels. Truly, these social chartists are no friend to the working man. Rather they would price his children out of honest employment.

Of course, the wealthy father did not need to put his children to work. But neither did he spend much quality time with them. He would employ a wicked governess to scare the children and their frail, sickly mother, who would die of embroidery at the age of thirty. The father would go on to have various illegitimate children by a succession of scullery maids, each of whom he would cast out in turn. Shunned and shamed, his former servants would die of melodrama in a rude shack. But one of the children would survive and run away to sea to work his passage on the coffin ships to Belgium. Years later, he would return to his father's estate to claim his rightful share of the inheritance, and would have to fight a duel on Salisbury Plain with his cruel half-brother who would cheat and fire before he had taken ten paces, thus accidentally shooting himself in the head. Meanwhile, their father had died in the mad-house for tax reasons and left no will, but a kindly old gentleman recognised our hero – who was about to hang mistakenly for the shooting of his half-brother – as the bastard son and rightful heir to the old squire's estate, but by now a car park had been built on it so they hanged him anyway.

All this changed with the First World War. A profound social shift occurred as women were drawn into heavy industry by the need for munitions. The war also altered once and for all the attitudes of men to their roles as fathers, because they were all killed. By the time a new generation had become fathers, it was the Depression and they were all unemployed so that was no good either but least it meant they were around more and could play with the kids. Then it was the Second World War, then post-war austerity and then the fifties.

The economic boom of the fifties and early sixties saw a dramatic growth in car-ownership. The motor car caused a huge change in the paternal role. One Sunday a month, the whole family would rise at six so that Father could take them on an outing. By noon he would have finished packing the hard-boiled eggs into the boot of the Vauxhall Victor and would arrange his children inside after weighing and numbering them. This was in the days before safety belts and gaps between the front seats, so five or six children could be seated uncomfortably next to their father in the front. Mother would travel in the back and navigate while trying to subdue Grandma who would be scaring the children with stories of a car accident she witnessed in 1936 and how the doctors couldn't tell which bits were the passengers and which bits were the knacker's horse. The children would take it in turns to get stung by wasps, be carsick and wet themselves but Father would refuse to stop until he reached the picnic site: a lay-by on a new stretch of dual carriageway. The picnic was eaten in the car to avoid the litter-bin full of angry hornets but the children were allowed out of the car to collect something for the school nature table. Father told them, 'If you're not back in five minutes, I'm leaving without you.' He was not serious, but would nonetheless drive off leaving one child behind. By the time the child was retrieved two hours later, he was hysterical and needed to be consoled, so the rest of the day was spent looking for an ice-cream van. It was after dark by the time Father delivered his brood safely home, tired but unhappy.

According to popular mythology, this period also saw the start of the collapse of family life. Since the fifties, children have been said to be wild, rebellious and lacking in respect. By implication, parents, and especially fathers, have not been doing enough to control them. Children no longer look up to the teacher or the local bobby, but this is because the teacher earns less than they get in pocket money and the bobby is under suspension for planting evidence.

Television is often blamed for the breakdown in discipline. The phrase 'Wait till your father gets home' no longer has any meaning. Father gets home, puts the telly on and falls asleep. It used to be considered to be his role to listen to a catalogue of offences from Mother and then take his belt to the children. This is what people mean when they say, 'We made our own entertainment in those days.' Nowadays, children have to learn about violence from videos.

The nineties have seen both worrying and encouraging developments in youth culture. On the one hand, we have seen teenagers walking around in flares. Too young to have been emotionally scarred by them the first time round, they have learned nothing from history. Those of us old enough to have lived through the 1970s never want to see anything like that happen again. On the positive side, I can remember when a hard lad's vital fashion accessory was steel toe-capped Dr Martens – today it's trainers, big, soft, bouncy trainers. It is completely impossible to kick someone's head in if you're wearing trainers.

Nonetheless, the youth seem to many to be out of control. The motor car is no longer associated with Sunday outings but with joy-riding. Is the breakdown of social order the result of fathers being called by their first names and the erosion of the idea that child abuse is character-building? Or have the young learned their morality from the smash-and-grab ethic of our economic system? And what of my generation of fathers, whose children's lives have only just begun? What can we expect from them? What can we do? Should we just get them to watch *The Simpsons* with us and hope they'll turn out all right? And what if we can't pick up Sky? Who will tape *The Simpsons* for us? Tracey and Pete? Yeah, they might, if we bought them some tapes. I'll ask them, they can only say no.[1]

Personally, I am not in favour of children calling their parents by their first names. This is not because I think it diminishes respect for elders or makes children experiment with crack. But I can't see the point of going through all the heartache, expense and exhaustion of bringing up kids if you don't even get to be called Daddy. We have a tendency today to forget that children are young and to treat them as adults with learning difficulties. Perhaps because the origins of human unhappiness are believed to be in our childhood, parents are becoming therapists, helping their children to get through childhood as quickly as possible. Babies are taken to gymnasia, toddlers instructed in the use of the word processor. If you have a fax machine wired up to a microwave, you can do your parenting from work. Maybe it's old-fashioned to think that men should give up work when their children are born. But if it's old-fashioned to think that work is a miserable, carcinogenic chain-gang leading to alienation, dyspepsia and the grave, then you can call me old-fashioned.

It almost seems that there is an unholy alliance between go-ahead parenting pioneers and Victorian bigots. The emphasis in education is shifting back to the idea that knowledge is something an adult inflicts upon a child, that information is no more than a series of individual, disconnected facts which have no meaning unless chanted in unison. The liberals are in retreat. There are psychotic howls of rage if an educationist dares to suggest that we should update the consciousness of children's books, or that old favourites like *Noddy Thrashes a Wog* aren't harmless bits of innocent fun.

This is not to say that all progress will be wiped out in

[1] If, like me, you haven't got a satellite dish, I recommend that you get to know Tracey and Pete, because they've got cable round their way.

a right-wing backlash. There are hopes for positive, tender fatherhood. Our shared sense of guilt about handing over to our children a world which is such a terrible shit-heap might encourage us to do all we can to make up for it. I should say at this point that I am not touting the philosophy which says that we are each individually responsible for the ecological disaster – I may have had the odd squirt under an arm but I'm not exactly ICI. Nonetheless, we know the kind of world we are bringing our children into and they do not ask to be born. Luckily my daughter's adopted so I get to feel totally blameless on that score.

Attitudes about how kids should be brought up go round in circles. Maybe we are not as modern as we think. Perhaps man is satisfying an ancient hunter-gatherer instinct when he stalks and brings down a pack of nappies with his bare hands. Maybe marking a child's height on the wall brings out the cave-painter in us. And how much of the joy of being the one to push the buggy derives from the damage we can do to other people's ankles? Perhaps fathers are, after all, fundamentally different from mothers. Then again, that stuff's all bollocks.[1]

Who knows how our children will judge our performance as fathers and as citizens of the Earth? We just have to do our best and not judge ourselves too harshly – unless we are bastards. But I shall conclude this chapter with my personal motto:

> We do not inherit the world from our parents, we borrow it from the building society.

---

[1] I should, at this juncture, question why I use testicles to mean 'nonsense', when I could equally have used ovaries, but I don't want to get into that now as the book's almost finished.

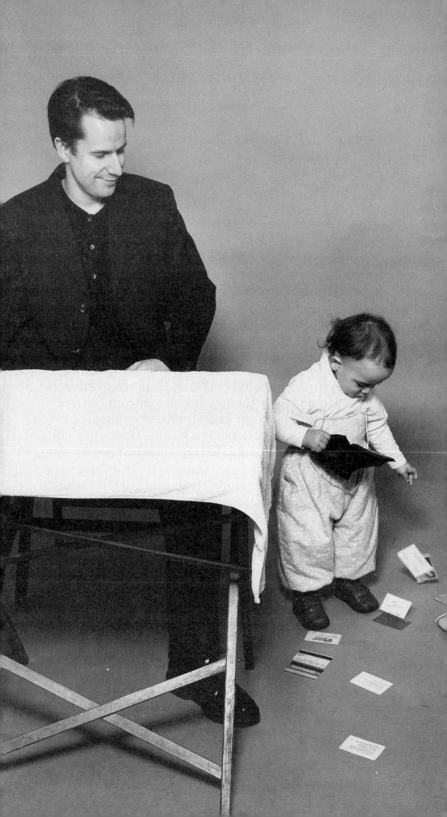

Author's Afterword

So that's my book. It's my first book, conceived in a moment of rashness, delivered late, and – I can't think of an analogy between writing and gestation.

Of course, the book one intends to write can be very different from the kind of book one ends up writing. When I sat down to write this book, I envisaged a lighthearted and irreverent but down-to-earth practical guide to the ups and downs of modern parenting, or a humorous, touching and essentially twee look at my own experiences as a father. It wasn't long, however, before I realised that what I was actually writing was an essay about the origins of the French Revolution, which in turn evolved into a letter to the *Radio Times*, a poem, a shopping list and a biography of Pia Zadora before finally emerging as the tense spy novel you see today.

I hope you've enjoyed reading my book as much as I enjoy overeating and thinking up tortures for brain-dead sports personalities who campaign for the Conservative Party. Writing a book is rather like fitting together the pieces of a jigsaw puzzle – it's best to bung it down any old how and then get on with something you like doing.

But you can't just scribble the first thing that comes into your head and expect it to be published, apparently. What you might think is a finished work your publisher calls 'a first draft', 'a synopsis', or 'a title'. There follow many long and painful hours and weeks before your publisher says the magic words, 'All right, I'll publish it, just let my family go.'

The cynical will say that every comedian at some stage knocks out a book, usually for the Christmas market. But my book is not intended as a stocking-filler, even though there was talk of publishing it in the shape of a leg, gift-wrapped and with a free tangerine attached.

Furthermore, I hope that the reader is not sitting on a lavatory in someone else's house, flicking through this after finishing all the cartoon books, and contemplating the fact that there's no toilet paper.

This will not be my last book. I don't know what my next book will be like but I can promise you this: I will not stoop to bringing out a book which is just a collection of old scripts from a television series – unless, that is, I've done a television series by then.

So what have I learned from the experience of writing my first book? And what advice can I give to someone who may be about to embark on the epic journey of writing a book for the first time? Well, above all, have fun – and DON'T PANIC!